VEGETABLE GARDENER'S HANDBOOK

The Art and Science of Vegetable Gardening Made Simple

Maxwell Greenfield

TABLE OF CONTENTS

INTRODUCTION

Welcome to "The Vegetable Gardener's Handbook," a comprehensive guide designed to transform your gardening journey into a fruitful and fulfilling adventure. As you embark on this green-thumbed voyage, you hold in your hands the key to unlocking the secrets of the soil, the mysteries of plant life, and the timeless wisdom of sustainable cultivation. This book is not just a collection of gardening techniques; it's an invitation to connect deeply with the earth, nurture life from the ground up, and partake in the age-old dance of growth and renewal that defines the essence of gardening.

Gardening is an art form, a science, and a meditation in motion. It's a practice that demands patience, fosters creativity, and rewards us with the simple joys of watching life unfold in sync with nature's rhythms. Whether you're a seasoned gardener with soil-etched hands or a novice with seeds of curiosity, this handbook is crafted to guide you through every step, from the initial survey of your garden space to the harvesting of your labor.

In the pages that follow, you'll find a treasure trove of knowledge distilled from the experience of seasoned gardeners, the latest research in horticulture, and the eternal wisdom that has been transmitted through generations. We begin with "Understanding Your Garden," a foundational chapter that prepares you to see your garden not just as a plot of land but as a vibrant ecosystem with its own unique characteristics and potential. Assessing your space, understanding the climate and seasonal variations, and selecting the right tools form the bedrock of successful gardening.

As we delve deeper, you'll uncover the secrets of "Soil Science for Gardeners," learning to appreciate the complex world beneath our feet that is so crucial to plant health. The chapters on composting and fertilization will equip you with the skills to nurture your soil organically, fostering a healthy, vibrant garden. Watering practices are then explored, emphasizing the art of giving life-sustaining moisture without waste or excess.

The heart of the handbook beats with the chapters dedicated to the cultivation of various vegetables and herbs. From the leafy greens of salads to the robust flavors of tomatoes, onions, and garlic, each chapter is designed to bring you closer to the dream of a bountiful, homegrown harvest. You'll learn not just how to plant and care for these staples but how to navigate the challenges of pests and diseases with resilience and organic solutions.

Seasonal gardening activities remind us that gardening is a year-round journey, with each season bringing its own tasks, challenges, and rewards. As we look beyond the confines of the vegetable patch, the final chapters encourage us to envision our gardens as bastions of sustainability, spaces that nourish our souls in addition to our bodies, support wildlife, and contribute to the health of our planet.

"The Vegetable Gardener's Handbook" is more than a manual; it's a manifesto for mindful living, a call to arms for those who wish to live in harmony with the earth. It's a guide for those who seek to turn their garden, regardless of its size, into a source of sustenance, joy, and inspiration. As you turn these pages, let them sow the seeds of a deeper connection with nature, a connection that grows and evolves with each season. Welcome to the journey. Welcome to the wonder. Welcome to the world of vegetable gardening.

CHAPTER 1
Understanding Your Garden

Assessing Your Space

Embarking on the journey of gardening begins with a critical yet often overlooked step: assessing your space. This initial phase is not merely about measuring dimensions or noting the presence of existing flora. It's about immersing yourself in the environment, understanding its unique attributes, and envisioning the potential that lies within. As you stand in your garden-to-be, you're not just a gardener; you're a steward of a piece of the earth, ready to coax from it beauty, sustenance, and life.

Assessing your space requires a blend of practicality and imagination. It's looking at the sunlight and seeing how it dances through the day, noting the areas bathed in light and those embraced by shade. Each ray of sunshine and shadow cast plays a crucial role in determining what will thrive in your garden. It's about feeling the soil, its texture, and its moisture and imagining the roots of future plants gripping this very earth. This tactile experience connects you to the ground, providing insights into what amendments it might need or what crops will flourish.

Beyond the physical attributes, assessing your space involves understanding the rhythm of the seasons in your corner of the world. It's recognizing the way the wind whispers through the trees and how water flows during a downpour. These elements guide where to plant, what to plant, and when to plant. They tell you where to erect barriers or windbreaks, where to create drainage, and where your garden will be most protected or exposed.

This phase is also about envisioning your space's potential. It's seeing beyond what's currently there and imagining what could be. Imagine rows of vibrant vegetables, patches of fragrant herbs, and trellises laden with climbing vines. It's about picturing yourself in this space through the seasons, tending to the plants, harvesting the fruits of your labor, and finding peace and satisfaction in the rhythm of gardening work.

But assessing your space is not a solitary step; it's a conversation with the land. It requires listening to what the environment tells you, respecting its limits, and working with its strengths. This dialogue forms the foundation of your gardening journey, grounding your efforts in the reality of your specific garden while opening up a world of possibilities.

In this chapter, we delve deep into the process of assessing your space, offering guidance on how to observe, measure, and plan. We provide strategies for mapping your garden, taking into account elements like water availability, soil type, and sunshine. We discuss how to set realistic goals based on your assessment, ensuring that your gardening endeavors are both fruitful and enjoyable. This chapter is your first step toward creating a garden that is not only a source of food and beauty but a sanctuary of learning, growth, and connection with nature.

Climate and Seasonal Considerations

Understanding the climate and seasonal considerations of your garden space is akin to learning the language of the land. This knowledge empowers you to communicate effectively with your environment, fostering a garden that not only survives but thrives. The climate defines the overarching environmental context in which your garden exists, shaping the life cycles of your plants, while the seasons dictate the rhythm of gardening activities throughout the year.

Climate encompasses more than just the average temperature of a location; it includes patterns of precipitation, wind, humidity, and extreme weather events. When choosing which plants are ideal for your landscape, each of these elements is crucial. For example, a region prone to drought will favor drought-tolerant species, whereas areas with abundant rainfall open the door to a wider variety of moisture-loving plants. Similarly, understanding your local climate zone provides invaluable insights into the growing season's length, guiding you in selecting plant varieties that will reach maturity within your area's unique temporal framework.

Seasonal considerations bring the concept of timing into focus. A number of crucial events occur during the gardening year: the final frost in the spring signals the safe planting of delicate crops; and for many species, the first frost of autumn marks the end of the growing season. These milestones, along with the shifting patterns of sunlight and temperature, dictate the rhythm of planting, maintenance, and harvest within the garden. By aligning your gardening activities with these natural cycles, you maximize the health and productivity of your plants.

Moreover, understanding the microclimates within your garden—a sun-soaked southern wall, a frost-prone low spot, or a wind-sheltered corner—allows for the strategic placement of plants, tailoring their location to match their environmental preferences. This nuanced understanding of climate and seasonality enables the gardener to orchestrate a symphony of growth where each plant is positioned to play to its strengths, contributing to a harmonious and bountiful garden.

In this chapter, we delve into strategies for assessing and adapting to your garden's climate and seasonal patterns. We explore how to leverage climate data, historical weather patterns, and on-site observations to make informed decisions about plant selection and garden planning. We discuss the importance of timing in the garden, from seasonal planting schedules to the strategic use of succession planting and crop rotation to enhance yield and soil health. By the end of this chapter, you will possess a deep understanding of how to work in tandem with the climate and seasons, turning environmental challenges into opportunities for garden success. This knowledge forms the cornerstone of a sustainable gardening practice, one that respects and responds to the natural world's rhythms and constraints.

Basic Gardening Tools and Equipment

Embarking on the gardening journey, one quickly learns that success blooms from the soil, nurtured by the skillful hands of the gardener and the essential tools of the trade. Basic gardening tools and equipment are the unsung heroes of the garden, each designed with a specific purpose in mind, from preparing the earth to planting seeds, nurturing growth, and harvesting the fruits of your labor. These tools are the bridge between the gardener's vision and the realization of a thriving garden.

Spade and Shovel

These tools are the foundation of garden work; they are indispensable for breaking ground, turning soil, and digging holes for new plants. A spade's sharp, flat blade is ideal for slicing through sod and edging beds, while a shovel, with its curved scoop, is perfect for moving soil, compost, and other bulk materials.

Garden Fork

More versatile than it appears, the garden fork is essential for loosening compacted soil, aerating the earth, and gently lifting plants. Its tines penetrate the soil with minimal disturbance, making it an invaluable tool for preparing beds for planting.

Hand Trowel

A gardener's best friend for transplanting bedding plants and herbs, digging small holes, and scooping soil into pots. It is ideal for detailed work and container gardening because to its small size and ease of maneuverability.

Hoe

The hoe is the gardener's ally in maintaining a weed-free garden. With a variety of shapes and sizes, the right hoe can effortlessly slice through the soil surface to uproot weeds, create furrows for seeding, and shape the soil around plants.

Rake

A rake, essential for smoothing soil and clearing debris, prepares the garden bed for planting. The flexible tines gather leaves and clippings, while a more robust rake is used to break up and even out the soil.

Pruners

Precision and care in pruning can shape a garden's aesthetic and health. Bypass pruners, with their scissor-like action, provide clean cuts on living plants, promoting healthy growth, while anvil pruners are suited for deadwood and harder materials.

Watering Can or Hose

Adequate watering is the lifeline of the garden. A watering can with a long spout offers control and gentleness for young plants, while a hose with a nozzle or sprinkler attachment can cover larger areas efficiently.

Wheelbarrow

For transporting soil, compost, garden tools, and harvest, a wheelbarrow saves time and back strain. Its design allows for the easy movement of heavy or bulky loads across the garden.

Gloves

Protecting the gardener's hands from thorns, splinters, and soil-borne pathogens, gloves are a fundamental piece of equipment. They range from lightweight and flexible for delicate tasks to heavy-duty for rough work.

Equipped with these basic tools, the gardener is well-prepared to face the myriad tasks the garden demands, from the first stirrings of spring to the final harvests of autumn. Each tool, an extension of the gardener's hand, is a testament to the timeless art of gardening, blending skill, care, and the joy of growing.

CHAPTER 2
Soil Science for Gardeners

Types of Soil

Soil is more than just the ground we walk on; it's a living, breathing foundation for all gardening efforts. Understanding the types of soil is a fundamental aspect of gardening that can greatly influence the success of your endeavors. The soil in your garden is a complex mixture of minerals, organic matter, water, and air, each contributing to the overall health of the plants you wish to grow. It acts as a reservoir for the nutrients, water, and air that your plants need to thrive. The three primary types of soil—sand, silt, and clay—form the basis of the countless variations gardeners might encounter.

Sandy soil is known for its coarse texture and quick drainage. Although it warms up quickly in the spring and permits planting early, certain plants may find it difficult to survive due to its poor ability to hold onto moisture and nutrients. Its large particles create gaps that allow water to flow through rapidly, often leaching essential nutrients away from plant roots. To improve sandy soil, one can incorporate organic matter, which helps retain both moisture and nutrients, thus providing a more hospitable environment for a wider variety of plants.

Silt soil, with its fine particles, feels smooth to the touch and retains water better than sandy soil. It holds nutrients well, making it fertile ground for many plants. However, its fine texture means it can compact easily, potentially hindering air and water movement. To prevent compaction, regular aeration and the addition of organic matter can increase its viability for plant growth, ensuring that roots receive adequate oxygen.

Clay soil is dense with very small, compact particles. While it's highly nutrient-rich, its fine texture means water drains slowly, leading to poor air circulation for plant roots and a risk of waterlogging. Working with clay soil requires patience; amending it with organic matter can improve drainage and aeration, making it more plant-friendly. The key is to enhance its structure gradually, allowing for better root growth and water movement.

Loam is often considered the ideal garden soil. This perfect blend of sand, silt, and clay combines the best characteristics of each soil type: it's fertile, well-draining, and retains moisture without compacting. Achieving loamy soil may require the addition of organic matter, sand, or other materials to balance out the existing soil's composition. Regular testing and amendments can help maintain its ideal structure and fertility.

Understanding these soil types allows gardeners to tailor their practices to suit their garden's specific needs. Whether amending the soil to alter its composition or choosing plants suited to the existing soil type, knowledge of the soil is a powerful tool in the gardener's toolkit. With this foundation, gardeners can create a thriving ecosystem that supports vibrant plant life, from the smallest flower to the largest vegetable patch. Soil science is not just an academic pursuit but a practical guide to unlocking the full potential of your garden and transforming it into a flourishing haven of biodiversity and beauty.

Soil Testing and Analysis

Soil testing and analysis stand as pivotal practices in the science of gardening, serving as the compass by which gardeners can navigate the nutritional landscape of their gardens. This process not only reveals the current state of the soil in terms of pH, nutrient levels, and organic matter content but also guides the amendments needed to cultivate a fertile environment for plants to thrive.

At the heart of soil testing is the pH level—a measure of the soil's acidity or alkalinity that significantly affects plant growth. Most plants flourish in soils with a pH level between 6.0 and 7.0, where essential nutrients are most readily available. A soil pH outside this range can hinder a plant's ability to absorb nutrients, regardless of the soil's richness in nutrients. With the help of testing kits that they can get from garden centers or extension services, gardeners can determine the pH of their soil and modify it by adding lime to raise it or sulfur to lower it, thus creating the ideal soil conditions for the plants they have chosen.

Beyond pH, soil tests evaluate crucial macronutrients: nitrogen (N), phosphorus (P), and potassium (K)—the N-P-K ratio found on fertilizer packages. These nutrients support plant growth in various ways, from root development to flowering and disease resistance. Understanding the existing levels of these and other nutrients like calcium, magnesium, and sulfur enables gardeners to select the appropriate type and amount of fertilizer, avoiding the pitfalls of over- or under-fertilization.

Organic matter content, another critical factor revealed through soil testing, influences soil structure, nutrient retention, moisture availability, and microbial activity. High organic matter improves soil structure, making it more friable and better at holding water and nutrients. This insight allows gardeners to enhance their soil with compost, manure, or other organic amendments, increasing the soil's ability to support healthy plant life.

Conducting a soil test is a simple yet profound act, requiring only a small sample of soil from the garden. This sample, sent to a laboratory, becomes the source of detailed information on the garden's current condition and its potential for improvement. The results, usually together with recommendations for amendments, provide a customized road map for enhancing the soil that is suitable for the goals of the gardener and the particular requirements of the garden.

Soil testing and analysis is a critical blend of science and creativity in gardening, enabling gardeners to tailor their approaches based on their garden's specific needs for better and more sustainable results. It's essential for maximizing garden potential and supporting plant growth.

SEE BONUS APPENDIX 1
CONDUCTING SOIL PH TESTS

Enhancing Soil Quality

Enhancing soil quality is a transformative journey that involves both science and intuition to create a thriving garden ecosystem. The foundation of a healthy garden lies not in the plants we see above ground but in the vibrant, living soil beneath. This chapter delves into the multifaceted approach to improving soil quality, focusing on organic matter enrichment, proper pH balance, and the introduction of beneficial organisms to foster a nutrient-rich environment conducive to plant growth.

Organic matter is the cornerstone of fertile soil, acting as a sponge that retains moisture and nutrients, thereby facilitating root penetration and aeration. The addition of compost, aged manure, leaf mold, or green manures from cover crops can significantly enhance the organic content of the soil. These amendments decompose over time, releasing nutrients slowly and feeding the soil's microbial life, which, in turn, supports plant health. This natural cycle mimics the nutrient recycling found in undisturbed ecosystems, providing a sustained release of nutrients as plants require them.

Balancing soil pH is another critical aspect of soil quality enhancement. The pH of the soil affects how many nutrients are available to plants; most nutrients are available in pH ranges between slightly acidic and neutral. Gardeners can adjust the soil's pH based on the results of a soil test. Lime can be added to acidic soils to raise their pH, while sulfur may be used to lower the pH of alkaline soils. This adjustment is not a one-time fix but a part of ongoing soil management, necessitating periodic retesting and amendment to maintain optimal conditions for plant growth.

Introducing beneficial organisms into the garden is akin to inviting nature's workforce to improve soil structure and nutrient availability. Earthworms, for example, are invaluable in aerating the soil and breaking down organic matter into plant-available forms. Similarly, the cultivation of mycorrhizal fungi relationships can enhance plant nutrient and water uptake, improving plant resilience against stress and disease. Incorporating biochar, a form of charcoal that provides habitat for microbial life, can further promote a healthy, living soil ecosystem.

Effective soil moisture management plays a pivotal role in soil quality. Adding organic materials to a mulch, like wood chips, straw, or leaves, can help retain moisture, limit weed growth, and eventually increase the amount of organic matter in the soil. The practice of crop rotation and the use of cover crops can prevent nutrient depletion and discourage the buildup of pests and diseases, further maintaining soil health.

In short, improving soil quality is an ongoing process that requires attention to the balance of nutrients, pH, organic matter, and living organisms in the soil. These practices help create fertile soil for healthy plant growth and benefit overall ecological health by following principles of sustainability and garden care.

SEE BONUS APPENDIX 2

HOW TO ADJUST PH

CHAPTER 3
The Art of Composting

Composting Basics

The art of composting transforms organic waste into gold for the garden, enriching soil with nutrients essential for plant growth. This chapter unravels the mysteries of composting, guiding gardeners through the basic principles of creating and maintaining a successful compost system. At its core, composting is a simple process, yet it harnesses complex ecological interactions to recycle kitchen scraps, yard waste, and other organic materials into a rich, earthy substance that enhances soil structure, fertility, and microbial life.

Composting starts with understanding the balance between carbon-rich "browns" and nitrogen-rich "greens." Brown materials, such as shredded paper, straw, and dried leaves, supply the carbon needed for the microbes that break down the compost. Greens, including fruit and vegetable scraps, coffee grounds, and fresh grass clippings, supply nitrogen, the critical component for building the protein that fuels microbial growth. The ideal ratio of browns to greens in a compost pile is roughly 30:1 by volume, a balance that encourages efficient decomposition without unpleasant odors.

Moisture and aeration are pivotal to the composting process. The pile should be moist as a wrung-out sponge to maintain microbial activity. Too much water suffocates the pile, slowing decomposition and leading to foul odors, while too little water halts microbial activity. Turning the pile regularly introduces oxygen, essential for aerobic decomposition and preventing the development of anaerobic conditions that can also produce undesirable smells.

The size of the compost pile impacts its ability to retain heat, with a volume of at least 3 feet by 3 feet by 3 feet recommended to generate sufficient internal heat for efficient decomposition. This heat is crucial for breaking down materials quickly and killing weed seeds and pathogens. However, composting is not a one-size-fits-all activity. Techniques can vary from simple heaps to sophisticated bin systems, worm composting (vermicomposting), and bokashi, a method of fermenting organic material. The choice of method depends on the gardener's space, time commitment, and the types of materials available for composting.

Over time, the compost pile undergoes a transformation as the materials break down into humus, the dark, nutrient-rich heart of compost. This process can take anywhere from a few months to over a year, depending on the conditions and materials involved. Gardeners can tell compost is ready when it's dark, crumbly, and has an earthy smell devoid of any original organic material's identity.

Incorporating finished compost into the garden revitalizes the soil, adding vital nutrients and improving its structure. Compost can be worked into garden beds, used as a top dressing for lawns and plants, or added to potting mixes. Beyond its physical benefits, composting is a sustainable practice that reduces waste, cuts greenhouse gas emissions from landfills, and fosters a deeper connection with nature's cycles.

By mastering the basics of composting, gardeners play an active role in soil stewardship, contributing to the health of their garden ecosystem and the planet. This chapter not only equips gardeners with the knowledge to start their composting journey but also inspires them to see waste as a valuable resource, turning leftovers into life for the garden.

Building Your Compost Pile

Constructing a compost pile is akin to crafting a layered masterpiece, where each component plays a critical role in transforming organic materials into nutrient-rich compost. The journey begins with selecting the right location—ideally, a spot that is both accessible and partially shaded to maintain moisture without the pile becoming too wet from direct rainfall. The ground beneath the compost pile should be bare earth, not only to enhance drainage but also to invite earthworms and beneficial microbes that accelerate the composting process.

The foundation of the compost pile is crucial. Start with a coarse layer of branches or straw a few inches deep. This layer promotes air circulation at the bottom of the pile, preventing compaction and ensuring that the materials do not become anaerobic, which can slow decomposition and produce undesirable odors.

Atop this base, begin adding organic materials in alternating layers of greens and browns. Greens are high-nitrogen elements that feed the microorganisms that break down the compost, like coffee grounds, kitchen trash, and recently cut grass. Browns, on the other hand, are carbon-rich materials like leaves, shredded paper, and straw, providing the microbes with energy to thrive. Maintaining a balance between these materials is key. An overabundance of nitrogen can cause a foul, overly wet pile, while too much carbon can slow down the composting process.

Water each layer lightly as it is added. The pile should be kept moist but not waterlogged, resembling the consistency of a wrung-out sponge. This moisture is essential for microbial activity but should be monitored, especially during dry spells or heavy rains.

Turning the pile is an integral part of building and maintaining it. Every few weeks, use a garden fork to turn the pile, moving material from the center to the outside and vice versa. This process aerates the pile, distributing air and moisture evenly, and helps to break up materials, speeding up decomposition. The act of turning also exposes any undecomposed materials to the pile's interior, where temperatures are higher due to microbial activity, ensuring that the composting process is thorough.

As the pile grows, monitor its temperature with a compost thermometer. In good condition, a compost pile will reach temperatures between 130°F and 160°F, the optimal range for decomposing materials and killing weed seeds and pathogens. This heat is a sign that the pile is actively composting. If the temperature does not rise, it may indicate a need for more nitrogen-rich materials, more moisture, or additional turning to incorporate oxygen.

Over time, the bottom and center of the pile will begin to transform into dark, crumbly compost, while the top and sides may still have recognizable materials. This is normal. Once a significant amount of the pile has decomposed, it can be sifted to separate the finished compost from larger, uncomposted pieces, which can be returned to a new pile to continue decomposing.

The process of building a compost pile is both an art and a science, requiring patience, observation, and adjustment. By following these guidelines, gardeners can create an autonomous system that recycles waste into a valuable resource, enriching their garden soil, supporting plant health, and contributing to a more sustainable world. This chapter not only guides the gardener through the practical steps of building a compost pile but also instills a deeper understanding of the composting process, empowering them to nurture their garden from the ground up.

Compost Maintenance and Usage

Maintaining a compost pile and harnessing its full potential requires ongoing attention and understanding. The process of compost maintenance is continuous, beginning from the moment the first layer is laid down to when the compost is finally ready to enrich the garden soil. This journey from raw organic material to nutrient-rich compost can be both rewarding and transformative, embodying the essence of recycling and sustainability.

As the compost pile evolves, its maintenance hinges on balance and observation. Regular monitoring of moisture levels is necessary, particularly during periods of severe weather. The compost should remain as damp as a wrung-out sponge. During dry spells, adding water to the pile may be necessary, whereas during rainy seasons, covering the pile might prevent it from becoming waterlogged. Air circulation is another critical factor; turning the pile every few weeks ensures that it receives the oxygen needed for aerobic decomposition. This activity not only aerates the pile but also mixes the layers, redistributing heat and microbes throughout.

Temperature monitoring serves as a gauge of the pile's health. A compost thermometer can be a valuable tool in this regard, helping to ensure that the pile reaches and maintains the temperatures necessary to break down materials effectively and kill off any seeds or pathogens. If the pile's temperature drops prematurely, it may require additional nitrogen-rich material or more frequent turning to reinvigorate the composting process.

The final stage of compost maintenance involves knowing when the compost is ready to use. Mature compost will be dark, crumbly, and have an earthy smell. It should bear no resemblance to the original materials. At this point, it can be sieved to remove any uncomposted items, which can be returned to a new pile for further decomposition. This finished product is a testament to the gardener's effort and nature's capacity to regenerate, ready to be used to improve soil structure, enhance moisture retention, and provide nutrients to plants.

Using compost effectively is as much an art as its creation. It can be spread as a top dressing for garden beds, mixed into the soil at planting time, or used as a component in potting mixes. Compost introduces beneficial microorganisms that help suppress plant diseases and pests, making it a cornerstone of organic gardening practices. In contrast to synthetic fertilizers, which can leach away fast, it also functions as a slow-release fertilizer, supplying nutrients gradually.

Composting completes the cycle of recycling organic waste in the garden and creates a stronger bond between people and the natural environment. It is a practice that enhances the gardener's understanding of the complex interplay between soil health, plant growth, and environmental sustainability. Through the diligent maintenance and thoughtful use of compost, gardeners can contribute to a healthier planet, one garden at a time, reinforcing the principle that in giving back to the earth, we enrich not just our gardens but also the broader ecosystem. This chapter, therefore, is not just a guide to composting but an invitation to engage in a practice that is both profoundly simple and deeply impactful, embodying the essence of sustainable gardening.

CHAPTER 4
Fertilization Fundamentals

Understanding Fertilizers

Knowing your fertilizers is key to gardening success since they supply the vital nutrients plants require to develop, thrive, and yield. The world of fertilizers can be complex, with a vast array of types, formulations, and application methods available. This chapter demystifies fertilizers, offering foundational knowledge that empowers gardeners to make informed choices that benefit their gardens and the environment.

At its core, fertilizer is a substance that is added to soil to supply one or more nutrients required for the healthy growth of plants. These nutrients are broadly categorized into macronutrients and micronutrients based on the quantities required by plants. Macronutrients, including nitrogen (N), phosphorus (P), and potassium (K), are needed in larger amounts and are often highlighted in fertilizer ratios (N-P-K). Nitrogen promotes leafy growth, phosphorus supports root development and flowering, and potassium enhances overall plant health. Micronutrients, such as iron, magnesium, and zinc, are needed in smaller quantities but are no less critical to plant development.

Fertilizers are also classified by their origin: organic and synthetic. Organic fertilizers are derived from natural sources, such as compost, manure, bone meal, or seaweed, and release nutrients slowly as they break down in the soil. This slow-release fosters steady, healthy growth and supports the soil's microbial life, enhancing soil structure and fertility over time. Synthetic fertilizers are manufactured chemically and offer nutrients in a more immediately available form. While they provide a quick nutrient boost, they do not improve soil health over the long term and can lead to nutrient runoff, potentially harming waterways.

Selecting the right fertilizer begins with understanding the specific needs of your garden. Soil tests are invaluable tools in this process, revealing nutrient deficiencies and guiding fertilizer choices. A garden that thrives or struggles can be determined by applying the right kind and quantity of fertilizer at the right time. Over-fertilization, particularly with synthetics, can harm plants and the environment, leading to nutrient leaching into groundwater and nearby aquatic systems.

The method and timing of fertilizer application are just as important as the type of fertilizer chosen. Granular fertilizers are applied to the soil and worked in around plants, releasing nutrients over time, while liquid fertilizers are diluted and applied directly to the soil or foliage, providing quicker nutrient uptake. Understanding the growth cycles of your plants will guide when to apply fertilizers—for instance, applying a high-phosphorus fertilizer to support blooming plants or a balanced fertilizer to maintain general garden health.

The role of fertilizers in the pursuit of a productive and sustainable garden cannot be overstated. By selecting appropriate fertilizers, applying them judiciously, and integrating them with practices that support soil health, gardeners can achieve lush, bountiful gardens that are resilient and environmentally friendly. This chapter not only aims to equip gardeners with the knowledge to navigate the complexities of fertilization but also to inspire an appreciation for the delicate balance between plant nutrition and ecosystem health, underscoring the importance of thoughtful, informed gardening practices.

Organic vs. Synthetic Fertilizers

In the realm of gardening, the debate between organic and synthetic fertilizers is as rich and complex as the soil we aim to enrich. This discussion delves into the essence of both fertilizer types, dissecting their benefits, drawbacks, and impacts on both gardens and the broader environment. Understanding the distinction between organic and synthetic fertilizers is not just about choosing a product; it's about aligning with a philosophy of gardening that respects the intricate web of life beneath our feet.

Organic fertilizers are derived from natural sources—plant, animal, or mineral. Examples include bone meal, blood meal, fish emulsion, and compost. The primary allure of organic options lies in their multifaceted benefits to the soil ecosystem. They improve soil structure, enhance water retention, and encourage the proliferation of beneficial microbes and earthworms. These fertilizers release nutrients slowly, matching more closely with plants' growth cycles. This gradual process minimizes the risk of over-fertilization and nutrient runoff, a common environmental concern associated with their synthetic counterparts. However, the nutrient ratios in organic fertilizers are often lower and more variable than in synthetics, which can make targeted nutrient management more challenging. Additionally, their slower release rates may not satisfy the immediate nutrient demands of fast-growing or nutrient-deficient plants.

Synthetic fertilizers, manufactured through chemical processes, offer precise nutrient ratios (N-P-K) and are designed for plants to release and absorb quickly. This immediate nutrient availability can be crucial for correcting deficiencies and supporting rapid growth phases. The predictability and control afforded by synthetic fertilizers are their main advantages, allowing gardeners to tailor their nutrient applications with precision. Yet, this strength is also a source of their main weakness. The rapid nutrient release can lead to leaching, where excess nutrients are washed away into waterways, contributing to pollution and eutrophication. Moreover, synthetic fertilizers do little to improve soil health over time; they may even degrade it by harming the microbial life crucial for soil vitality.

The choice between organic and synthetic fertilizers transcends simple gardening decisions, touching upon broader themes of environmental stewardship and sustainability. Organic fertilizers, with their slow-release properties and soil-enhancing benefits, embody a holistic approach to gardening that nurtures not just the plants but the entire ecosystem. In contrast, synthetic fertilizers offer a more targeted, immediate solution to nutrient deficiencies, albeit with potential long-term environmental costs.

As gardeners, our actions echo in the health of our gardens and the environment at large. Whether we lean towards organic or synthetic fertilizers, the key lies in using them responsibly and judiciously. By understanding the specific needs of our gardens, the life cycles of our plants, and the long-term impacts of our choices, we can cultivate gardens that are not only productive and beautiful but also harmonious with the natural world. This chapter strives to equip gardeners with the knowledge to navigate the complex world of fertilization thoughtfully, blending science with a deep respect for nature, to foster gardens that thrive sustainably.

Application Techniques

The art of fertilization is akin to a nuanced dance between the gardener and the garden, where timing, technique, and type of fertilizer play pivotal roles in nurturing plant health and soil vitality. This chapter delved into the multifaceted world of fertilizer application techniques, shedding light on how to nourish your garden effectively. This exploration is not merely about dispensing nutrients; it's about fostering a deep-rooted connection with the earth and ensuring its flourishing for generations to come.

Understanding the nuances of fertilizer application begins with recognizing that different plants have unique nutritional needs throughout their growth cycles. The cornerstone of effective fertilization lies in the method of application—whether broadcasting, side-dressing, foliar feeding, or utilizing slow-release formulas. Each technique has its own set of advantages tailored to meet specific requirements, ensuring that plants receive the right nutrients at the right time.

Broadcasting involves the even spreading of fertilizer over a large area before tilling or planting. This method is particularly beneficial for preparing new beds or lawns, as it ensures a uniform distribution of nutrients across the entire planting area. However, careful calculation is required to avoid nutrient runoff, which can be detrimental to nearby water sources.

Side-dressing, on the other hand, refers to the application of fertilizer alongside growing plants. This targeted approach delivers nutrients directly to the root zone of established plants, providing a timely boost during critical growth phases. Side-dressing is especially useful for heavy feeders or crops that benefit from mid-season nutrient replenishment.

Foliar feeding involves the spraying of liquid fertilizer directly onto the leaves of plants. This method allows for rapid absorption of nutrients through the stomata, offering a quick remedy for nutrient deficiencies. While not a substitute for soil fertilization, foliar feeding can be an effective way to address specific nutritional needs or stress recovery.

Slow-release fertilizers, whether organic or synthetic, are designed to dispense nutrients over an extended period of time gradually. This controlled release mimics natural soil processes, reducing the risk of over-fertilization and nutrient leaching. Incorporating slow-release fertilizers into the soil at planting time ensures a steady supply of nutrients, supporting sustained growth and reducing the need for frequent applications.

In addition to these methods, the incorporation of compost and other organic matter into the soil acts as both a fertilizer and a soil conditioner. This practice enhances soil structure, improves water retention, and encourages the activity of beneficial microorganisms, all of which contribute to the holistic health of the garden ecosystem.

The successful application of fertilizers also hinges on understanding the soil's pH and nutrient levels, which can be determined through soil testing. Adjusting fertilization practices based on soil test results ensures that plants receive the appropriate nutrients in the correct proportions, thereby maximizing growth potential and minimizing environmental impact.

Ultimately, the fundamentals of fertilization transcend the act of nutrient application. They embody a philosophy of mindful stewardship, where the gardener's hand guides the garden's growth in harmony with nature's rhythms. Through the thoughtful application of fertilizers, we not only nourish our plants but also cultivate a legacy of sustainability and abundance within our gardens. This chapter aims to empower gardeners with the knowledge and techniques to skillfully navigate the complexities of fertilization, fostering lush, vibrant gardens that thrive in concert with the natural world.

SEE BONUS APPENDIX 3
PRACTICAL TIPS IN THE USE OF FERTILIZERS

CHAPTER 5
Watering Your Garden

Efficient Watering Practices

Learning to water your garden effectively is similar to learning how to do a delicate skill where life is given to the garden's core, drop by drop. This chapter delves deep into the realm of sophisticated irrigation strategies, aiming to equip gardeners with the wisdom to water their gardens not just adequately but optimally. The goal is to transcend mere survival, enabling each plant to thrive, bloom, and bear fruit in its full glory, all the while conserving one of our planet's most precious resources: water.

Efficient watering is founded on the understanding that not all water delivery methods are created equal and that the needs of the garden vary dramatically across different stages of plant growth, types of plants, and environmental conditions. To water efficiently, one must tailor the watering approach meticulously to the unique requirements of each garden, ensuring that every drop of water serves its purpose fully.

The first step towards efficient watering is recognizing the importance of timing. Watering in the early morning reduces evaporation and allows water to penetrate deeply into the soil, reaching the roots where it's most needed. Evening watering is less ideal due to the potential for moisture to remain on the leaves overnight, which can lead to fungal diseases. The timing of watering, therefore, plays a crucial role in both plant health and water conservation.

The amount of water applied is equally critical. Over-watering can be just as detrimental as under-watering, leading to root rot, nutrient leaching, and wasteful runoff. The key is to provide enough water to moisten the root zone, encouraging robust root growth without saturating the soil beyond what the plants can use. Utilizing moisture meters or the simple finger test can help gardeners gauge the soil's moisture level accurately, ensuring plants receive the perfect amount of hydration.

Moreover, the method of water delivery can significantly impact the efficiency of watering practices. Drip irrigation systems and soaker hoses are champions of water conservation, delivering water directly to the base of plants, minimizing waste, and reducing evaporation. These systems can be adjusted to meet the specific needs of each plant, ensuring that water is used judiciously and effectively.

In addition to these techniques, mulching around plants serves multiple purposes. It helps retain soil moisture, reduces water evaporation, keeps soil temperatures consistent, and adds an extra layer of defense against water-thirsty weeds. Mulching is a simple yet powerful ally in the quest for efficient watering.

Efficient watering also involves understanding the garden's ecosystem. Recognizing the signs of water stress in plants, changing irrigation schedules in response to the weather, and being mindful of the water needs of different plants are all integral parts of a holistic approach to garden watering.

In this chapter, we unfold the layers of knowledge and practice that comprise efficient watering practices. From the technical precision of irrigation systems to the intuitive understanding of plant and soil needs, we guide the reader through a comprehensive exploration of how to water wisely and well. This journey is not just about sustaining life in the garden but about nurturing a thriving, resilient, and water-wise oasis that reflects the gardener's care, respect for nature, and commitment to sustainability. Through mastering efficient watering practices, we not only enhance the beauty and bounty of our gardens but also contribute to the stewardship of our planet's vital water resources.

SEE BONUS APPENDIX 4
HOW TO MAKE A GOOD MULCH

Drip Irrigation and Soaker Hoses

In the verdant world of gardening, the advent of drip irrigation and soaker hoses marks a pivotal shift towards sustainable and precise watering techniques. This chapter delves into the nuanced realms of these innovative systems, shedding light on their significance in the modern garden and how they redefine the essence of nurturing plant life.

Drip irrigation shows itself to be a highly effective method, meticulously designed to deliver water directly to the base of the plant. This method is the epitome of precision, ensuring that every drop of water is utilized to its fullest potential and significantly reducing waste. Its implementation in the garden invites a symphony of benefits, including the minimization of evaporation and the elimination of runoff, making it an ideal choice for regions grappling with water scarcity.

The mechanism behind drip irrigation is both simple and ingenious. Through a network of valves, tubes, and emitters, water drips slowly to the roots of plants, providing a steady supply of moisture that meets the plants' needs without oversaturation. This targeted approach not only conserves water but also fosters a healthier plant environment by reducing the humidity levels around the foliage, thereby curtailing the prevalence of leaf diseases.

Soaker hoses, with their porous design, complement the drip system by providing a more generalized yet equally efficient method of watering. Laid out along the rows of plants or wrapped around them, these hoses seep water gradually into the soil, reaching the roots without any splash back or erosion. They are especially beneficial in densely planted beds, where their gentle weeping ensures that water seeps uniformly, catering to each plant's hydration needs.

The integration of drip irrigation and soaker hoses into the garden's watering regime is not merely a matter of utility but a reflection of a deeper understanding of the garden's ecological balance. It represents a commitment to nurturing the garden in harmony with nature, minimizing the environmental footprint while maximizing the garden's potential for growth and productivity.

Moreover, these systems offer gardeners the flexibility to customize watering schedules to the specific needs of different plants, accommodating a wide range of water requirements. This level of control is invaluable in creating a diverse and thriving garden where each plant, from the robust tomato to the delicate lettuce, receives the precise amount of water it needs to flourish.

The transition to drip irrigation and soaker hoses is more than just an upgrade in garden technology; it is an evolution in gardening philosophy. It speaks to the gardener's role as a steward of the earth, responsible for using resources wisely and with foresight. This chapter guides the reader through the practical aspects of installing and operating these systems, but more importantly, it aims to instill a mindset of mindful watering practices that resonate with the values of sustainability and reverence for the environment.

In embracing drip irrigation and soaker hoses, gardeners embark on a journey of discovery, learning to listen to the subtle cues of the garden and respond with a nurturing touch that is both gentle and efficient. This chapter, therefore, is not just a manual on watering techniques but a manifesto for a deeper, more intuitive engagement with the garden, where every drop of water becomes a testament to the gardener's commitment to cultivating life in its most vibrant form.

Dealing with Drought Conditions

Navigating the challenges of drought conditions in the garden requires a blend of innovation, strategy, and a deep understanding of the natural world. This chapter delves into the essence of cultivating a thriving garden under the harsh constraints of water scarcity, offering a beacon of hope and a roadmap for resilience in the face of environmental adversity.

Drought conditions test the mettle of even the most seasoned gardeners, presenting a scenario where every drop of water is precious and the margin for error is slim. Under these circumstances, the art of gardening transforms into a science, where knowledge, patience, and adaptability become the tools for ensuring the survival and prosperity of the garden.

The cornerstone of drought-resistant gardening lies in the soil. Enhancing soil quality with organic matter such as compost not only improves its water-holding capacity but also encourages deeper root growth, enabling plants to access moisture from further below the surface. Mulching plays a pivotal role, acting as a protective blanket that reduces evaporation, keeps the soil cool, and suppresses weed growth that would otherwise compete for water.

Watering practices must be meticulously planned and executed with precision. Early morning or late evening watering reduces water loss to evaporation, allowing more water to penetrate the soil and reach the roots. Utilizing soaker hoses and drip irrigation systems maximizes efficiency, delivering water directly to the base of the plants where it's needed most, minimizing waste, and ensuring that every drop contributes to the well-being of the garden.

Choosing the right plants is critical in a drought-prone garden. Drought-tolerant species, native plants, and those with deep root systems are more adept at surviving in arid conditions. These plants have evolved to thrive with minimal water, making them ideal candidates for a garden designed to withstand the challenges of drought.

Rainwater harvesting presents a sustainable solution, capturing rainwater from rooftops and storing it for future use in the garden. This not only provides a free source of water but also reduces dependency on municipal systems, aligning the garden more closely with the cycles of nature.

In times of drought, gardeners must also be willing to prioritize, focusing water on the most critical areas and plants. It may mean making tough choices, such as sacrificing annuals to save perennials, trees, and shrubs that represent a longer-term investment in the garden's ecosystem.

Dealing with drought conditions is not merely about survival; it's about adapting and thriving. This chapter offers not just strategies and techniques but a philosophy of gardening that respects and works within the limits of the natural environment. It's a testament to the gardener's resilience, creativity, and unwavering commitment to nurturing life, even in the face of adversity.

Through a combination of soil management, efficient watering practices, strategic plant selection, and innovative water conservation methods, gardeners can navigate the challenges of drought, ensuring that their gardens remain a source of beauty, sustenance, and joy, regardless of the climatic conditions. This chapter is a guide to building not just a drought-resistant garden but a testament to the enduring spirit of growth, resilience, and harmony with nature.

CHAPTER 6
Cultivating Salads

Growing Different Types of Lettuce

The cultivation of lettuce, a cornerstone of salad gardening, represents a symphony of variety, each type bringing its own unique texture, flavor, and color to the garden and plate. This chapter begins a thorough investigation of the varied world of lettuce, guiding the gardener through the nuances of growing crisp Iceberg, buttery Bibb, flavorful Romaine, and the delicate leaves of loose-leaf varieties. Lettuce, with its wide range of types, is not just a crop; it's a canvas for creativity and a testament to the gardener's skill in nurturing the earth's bounty.

Understanding the temperament and needs of different lettuce varieties is paramount. Iceberg, with its crispness, thrives in cooler conditions, hinting at the need for strategic planting to avoid the midsummer heat. The tender Bibb lettuce, a variety that demands attention to soil moisture and gentle care, rewards the gardener with leaves of unparalleled softness. Romaine, known for its robustness, offers not just depth of flavor but also versatility, thriving in a range of conditions and offering sustenance beyond the salad bowl into the heart of culinary creations.

Loose-leaf lettuces, with their ease of cultivation and continuous harvest, encourage a garden of perpetual greenery. Their resilience and rapid growth make them ideal for those seeking both efficiency and yield in their gardening endeavors. With each leaf picked, a new one emerges, symbolizing the cycle of growth and the perpetual promise of the garden.

Cultivating lettuce requires more than just planting seeds; it demands an understanding of the rhythm of the seasons. Succession planting, the practice of planting seeds at intervals, ensures a continuous harvest, turning the garden into a living larder that provides fresh lettuce throughout the growing season. This technique, coupled with an awareness of each variety's preference for sun and shade, allows the gardener to navigate the changing moods of the weather, ensuring that every lettuce plant reaches its full potential.

The chapter explores the intricacies of soil preparation, stressing the significance of organic matter-enriched, well-draining soil for fostering robust root and leaf development. Watering practices are tailored to lettuce's needs, focusing on maintaining consistent soil moisture without waterlogging to foster tender leaves and prevent bitterness.

Pest management is addressed with the understanding that the best defense is a healthy plant. Encouraging biodiversity, employing barrier methods, and practicing crop rotation are strategies highlighted to keep common adversaries at bay, ensuring that the lettuce garden remains a place of abundance rather than a battleground.

In the world of lettuce cultivation, the gardener becomes a conductor, orchestrating the elements of soil, water, and care to create a symphony of flavors, textures, and colors. This chapter is not just a guide but an invitation to engage deeply with the earth and its cycles, to appreciate the diversity of lettuce, and to celebrate the joy of harvesting a crisp leaf straight from the garden. It's a testament to the fact that, with knowledge, care, and respect for nature, the humble act of growing lettuce can become an art form, enriching both the garden and the soul.

Caring for Spinach and Arugula

In the verdant realm of salad gardening, the cultivation of spinach and arugula stands out as a testament to the gardener's dedication to both flavor and nutrition. These leafy greens, with their distinct tastes and textures, bring vitality to the garden and diversity to the table. This chapter delves into the nuanced art of nurturing these crops, guiding the gardener through each step, from soil preparation to harvest, with an emphasis on organic practices that respect and enhance the natural environment.

Spinach, with its rich, earthy flavor, thrives in excellent conditions, making it a perfect candidate for early spring or late fall planting. Its preference for well-drained, fertile soil rich in organic matter sets the stage for the gardener's initial tasks: soil amendment and site selection. The application of a balanced, organic compost prior to planting ensures a nutrient-rich foundation that supports robust growth. Watering practices for spinach require a delicate balance, providing enough moisture to sustain growth while avoiding soggy conditions that can lead to root rot and disease.

Arugula, on the other hand, brings a peppery zest to the salad bowl and is slightly more forgiving in its cultivation requirements. Its adaptability to a range of soil conditions and its rapid growth make it an excellent choice for gardeners looking to enjoy quick harvests. Like spinach, arugula benefits from soil enriched with organic compost, but it is more tolerant of dry conditions, making efficient water management a less critical concern. However, to achieve the tender leaves desired in salad greens, consistent moisture and regular harvesting are recommended.

Mulching plays a crucial role in the care of both spinach and arugula, helping to retain soil moisture, regulate temperature, and suppress weed growth. An organic mulch, such as straw or shredded leaves, not only contributes to the health of the soil but also reduces the need for frequent watering, making it an essential component of water-wise gardening.

Pest management in the cultivation of spinach and arugula emphasizes preventative measures and organic interventions. Crop rotation, companion planting, and the encouragement of beneficial insects are strategies employed to maintain balance in the garden and deter pests. Should challenges arise, organic solutions, such as neem oil or insecticidal soap, are preferred and applied judiciously to minimize impact on non-target species and the broader ecosystem.

Harvesting these greens at their peak of freshness ensures the highest nutritional value and the best flavor. Spinach, harvested when the leaves are tender and vibrant, offers versatility in both raw and cooked applications. Arugula, often harvested while young and tender brings a bold flavor to salads, sandwiches, and more. The practice of cut-and-come-again harvesting extends the productive life of these plants, providing gardeners with a sustained yield throughout the growing season.

In caring for spinach and arugula, the gardener engages in a process that is both a science and an art. Attention to detail, from soil preparation to pest management, reflects a deep respect for the natural world and a commitment to sustainable gardening practices. These leafy greens, with their myriad health benefits and culinary applications, embody the rewards of this dedication, enriching our gardens, our kitchens, and our well-being.

SEE BONUS APPENDIX 5

THE DIFFERENT KINDS OF SALADS

Harvesting and Storage Tips

The careful procedure of gathering and storing these lush jewels represents the pinnacle of creating salads, where the verdant efforts of a gardener's labor shift from soil to table. This chapter unravels the nuances of harvesting salad greens, with a focus on ensuring that the vitality of lettuce, spinach, arugula, and other salad staples is preserved from garden to plate. Delving into this critical phase, we explore strategies that sustain the crispness and nutritional integrity of each leaf, ensuring that gardeners can enjoy the fruits of their labor at the peak of freshness.

Harvesting salad greens is an art that balances timing and technique to capture the essence of each plant. For many leafy greens, the early morning offers an ideal harvest time, when leaves are most hydrated, and temperatures are cool. This practice prevents wilting and preserves the crisp texture that is coveted in salad ingredients. Gardeners are recommended to carefully trim leaves with clean, sharp shears or scissors, making sure to keep the plant's root intact to promote more growth. This method, often referred to as "cut-and-come-again," maximizes yield and extends the harvesting window.

The storage of salad greens post-harvest is pivotal in maintaining their quality. Immediate cooling is essential to halt the degradation process, with the use of cold-water baths serving dual purposes: it cools the greens. It removes any residual soil or garden debris. After a gentle yet thorough washing, leaves should be dried as much as possible. Salad spinners excel in this role, removing excess water without damaging the tender leaves. Moisture is the adversary of stored greens, leading to rapid spoilage. Thus, wrapped loosely in a dry, clean cloth or paper towel to absorb any remaining moisture, the greens are then placed in a perforated plastic bag or container. This setup allows for air circulation while maintaining a humid environment, which is crucial for preserving freshness.

Refrigeration plays a crucial role in extending the shelf life of salad greens. Stored in the crisper drawer of a refrigerator, the optimal temperature range is between 32°F and 36°F (0°C to 2°C). This chilly, controlled climate slows the respiration rate of the greens, reducing water loss and nutrient degradation. Under these conditions, most salad greens can maintain their quality for up to a week, though the sooner they are consumed, the better their flavor and nutritional content.

Innovative storage solutions, such as vacuum-sealed containers, offer an alternative method for preserving greens longer by reducing their exposure to air, which can accelerate spoilage. However, the simplicity of a breathable bag and the careful balance of humidity often yield equally satisfactory results without the need for specialized equipment.

In synthesizing these practices, gardeners forge a connection between the earth and the table, ensuring that the vibrancy of their gardens is reflected in the meals they serve. The meticulous care given to the harvesting and storage of salad greens not only maximizes the enjoyment of these nutritious, flavorful crops but also honors the time and effort invested in their cultivation. Through this careful stewardship, the garden becomes more than a source of sustenance; it is a testament to the cyclical beauty of growth, harvest, and renewal.

CHAPTER 7
Tomato Gardening

Planting and Supporting Tomato Plants

Tomato gardening is a venture that combines the science of horticulture with the art of nurturing. Planting tomatoes requires attention to detail from the get-go. Begin by choosing a site that receives at least six to eight hours of sunlight per day. Tomatoes thrive in warm conditions, so plant outside just after the risk of frost has passed. The soil should be rich, well-draining, and amended with compost to provide the nutrients these voracious feeders require.

Starting tomatoes from seeds indoors about 6–8 weeks before the last expected frost gives you a head start on the growing season. Use a light, seed-starting mix and keep the soil moist but not waterlogged. Seedlings are ready to be moved into separate pots once they have grown their second set of genuine leaves.

Hardening off is critical before transplanting outdoors; gradually acclimate your tomato plants to outdoor conditions over a week to reduce shock. When planting, bury two-thirds of the plant, including the stem, as this encourages the formation of additional roots, bolstering both support and nutrient uptake.

Tomato plants demand support to thrive. Options include cages, stakes, or trellises, chosen based on the variety of tomatoes and your garden space. Determinate (bush) types are more compact and often do well with cages, while indeterminate (vining) varieties can reach several feet and are best supported by staking or trellising. Install supports when planting to avoid disturbing the roots later on.

Proper spacing is crucial to allow for air circulation and reduce disease risk; generally, leave 24-36 inches between plants and 3-4 feet between rows, adjusting based on the specific variety's growth habits. Mulching around the plants helps retain soil moisture, regulate temperatures, and reduce weed competition.

Irrigation should be consistent, aiming for the base to keep foliage dry and minimize disease exposure. A drip irrigation system or soaker hoses are ideal for delivering water directly to the soil and roots without wetting the leaves.

Companion planting can be beneficial for tomatoes. Marigolds, basil, and nasturtiums can deter pests, while carrots can help aerate the soil around them. However, avoid planting tomatoes near potatoes or brassicas, as they can share diseases and pests.

Monitoring for pests and diseases is ongoing. Regularly check your plants and act swiftly to mitigate issues using organic or recommended treatments. Pruning, particularly for indeterminate varieties, helps to focus the plant's energy on fruit production rather than excessive foliage growth.

In essence, the technicalities of tomato gardening—from the careful preparation of soil and strategic planting to diplomatic support and vigilant care—compose a narrative of cultivation that rewards the gardener with a rich bounty of succulent tomatoes.

SEE BONUS APPENDIX 6
THE VARIOUS TYPES OF TOMATOES

Pest and Disease Management in Tomato Gardening

Managing pests and diseases is a critical aspect of tomato gardening, ensuring the health and productivity of your plants. Effective management strategies begin with prevention, employing practices that reduce the risk of infestation and spread. Regular monitoring is essential to identify problems early, allowing for timely intervention.

Preventive Measures:

Crop Rotation: Avoid planting tomatoes in the same location year after year. Rotating crops helps break the life cycles of pests and diseases, reducing their presence in the soil.

Sanitation: Keep the garden free of debris and weeds, which can harbor pests and diseases. Remove and destroy infected plants or plant parts immediately to prevent the spread of disease.

Proper Spacing: Ensure adequate spacing between tomato plants to improve air circulation. This practice helps reduce the humidity around the plants, making them less susceptible to fungal diseases.

Mulching: Apply a layer of organic mulch around tomato plants to prevent soil-borne pathogens from splashing onto leaves during watering or rain.

Water Management: Water plants at the base to avoid wetting the foliage, which can promote fungal diseases. Consider drip irrigation or soaker hoses to minimize water contact with leaves.

Identifying and Managing Common Pests:

Tomato Hornworms: Large green caterpillars that feed on leaves and fruit. Remove by hand from plants. Introduce natural predators like ladybugs and parasitic wasps to your garden.

Aphids: Small pests that suck plant sap, weakening plants. Use a strong jet of water to knock them off plants, or apply insecticidal soap.

Identifying and Managing Common Diseases:

Early Blight and Late Blight: Fungal diseases causing leaf spots and plant decay. Practice crop rotation and remove affected foliage. Apply fungicides as a last resort, following organic options first.

Bacterial Spot and Speck: Causes small, dark spots on leaves and fruit. Use disease-resistant tomato varieties and avoid overhead watering.

Companion Planting for Pest and Disease Control:

Planting basil near tomatoes can repel flies and mosquitoes, while marigolds deter nematodes and other pests. Garlic and onions planted around tomato plants can help repel aphids and prevent fungal diseases.

Monitoring and Intervention:

Regular inspection of tomato plants is critical to early detection of pests and diseases. Examine plants weekly for signs of stress, damage, or disease and take immediate action to mitigate problems. Use organic pesticides and fungicides, when necessary, always following label instructions for application rates and safety precautions.

In summary, successful pest and disease management in tomato gardening involves a combination of preventative measures, regular monitoring, and timely intervention. By adopting these strategies, gardeners can minimize the impact of pests and diseases on their tomato crops, leading to a bountiful harvest.

Harvesting and Pruning Techniques for Tomato Gardening

Harvesting and pruning are essential techniques in tomato gardening that influence both the yield and health of your plants. Mastering these practices ensures a bountiful harvest of quality tomatoes and maintains vigorous plant growth throughout the season.

Harvesting Techniques:

Tomatoes should be harvested when they are firm and have reached their full color, which varies depending on the variety. This could range from deep reds to yellows, oranges, or even purples. Use a clean, sharp pair of scissors to cut the stem close to the fruit or gently twist the tomato off the vine. Harvesting in the morning can result in crisper, more flavorful tomatoes.

For varieties that ripen at different times, regular harvesting encourages the plant to produce more fruit. If frost threatens before all the tomatoes have ripened, you can harvest the green tomatoes and ripen them indoors at a temperature between 60° and 70°F in a dark place. Wrapping them in paper can accelerate the ripening process.

Pruning Techniques:

Indeterminate tomato cultivars are the main targets of pruning since they bear fruit all season long. Determinate varieties, which grow to a specific size and produce all their fruit at once, require minimal pruning.

- **Remove Suckers**: Suckers are tiny shoots that emerge in the axils between the stems and the leaves. Removing these when they are small, about 2-4 inches, helps direct the plant's energy into fruit production rather than vegetative growth. Pinch them off with your fingers, or use a sharp pair of scissors.

- **Top the Plant**: As the end of the growing season approaches or the plant reaches the top of its support structure, remove the top growth tip. This encourages the plant to stop growing upward and focus on ripening the existing fruit.

- **Thin Leaves to Improve Airflow**: Removing some of the older leaves, especially those touching the ground or densely packed, can improve air circulation around the plant. This helps to reduce the humidity around the foliage, lowering the risk of fungal diseases.

- **Prune to a Few Main Stems**: Pruning the plant to keep two to three main stems will help increase air circulation and sunshine penetration, which will benefit indeterminate varieties in particular and result in healthier plants and tastier fruit.

Transplanting Distance for Pruning Efficiency:

When planting, consider the pruning strategy you plan to use. For intensive pruning, plants can be spaced closer together, about 18–24 inches apart, because the pruning will reduce the plant's overall size. For minimal pruning, allow more space, about 24-36 inches, to ensure adequate airflow and light penetration.

Properly executed harvesting and pruning techniques will significantly impact the productivity and health of your tomato plants, resulting in an abundant and prolonged harvest season.

CHAPTER 8
Onions and Garlic

Cultivating Onions

Cultivating onions is a rewarding endeavor for any gardener, yielding bulbs that are fundamental to cuisines worldwide. Success in onion cultivation hinges on understanding their growth requirements and lifecycle. Biennial onions usually are cultivated as annuals, and the length of the day affects how they develop. There are three types of onions: day-neutral, long-day, and short-day, each of which is suitable for a particular latitude.

Soil Preparation and Planting: Onions demand well-drained, fertile soil with a pH of 6.0 to 7.5. Prior to planting, incorporate plenty of organic matter and a balanced fertilizer into the soil to promote healthy growth. Transplants, sets (small bulbs), or seeds can all be used to grow onions. Seeds should be started indoors 6–8 weeks before the last frost date. For direct sowing, do so as soon as the soil is workable. Sets and transplants should be planted after the danger of frost has passed, typically spaced 4-6 inches apart in rows 12–18 inches apart.

Watering and Nutrition: Consistent moisture is crucial for onions, requiring about 1 inch of water per week, either from rainfall or irrigation. Avoid overhead watering to minimize disease risk. Fertilize with a nitrogen-rich formula about three weeks after planting and again when the bulbs begin to form to encourage bulb enlargement rather than leaf growth.

Weed and Pest Management: Onions are relatively low-maintenance but keep the planting area free from weeds, which can compete for nutrients and water. Straw or other organic material mulching can help keep the soil moist and reduce weed growth. Common pests include onion thrips and the onion maggot. Control measures include crop rotation, using reflective mulch to deter thrips, and applying appropriate insecticides if necessary.

Harvesting: Onions are ready to harvest when the tops begin to fall over and yellow, typically in late summer. Gently lift the bulbs with a fork, being careful not to damage them. Allow the onions to dry or cure in a warm, airy location for 2-3 weeks until the outer skins are papery. This curing process is essential for storage longevity.

Storage: After curing, trim the roots and cut back the tops to about an inch. Store onions in a cool, dry place with good air circulation. Properly cured onions can be stored for several months, depending on the variety.

Companion Planting: Plant onions alongside carrots, beets, and cabbage family crops to deter common pests. However, avoid planting onions near peas and beans, as they can inhibit each other's growth.

In summary, successful onion cultivation requires attention to soil preparation, correct spacing, consistent watering, and vigilant pest management. With proper care, onions will thrive and produce a bountiful harvest ready for the kitchen or storage.

Growing Garlic Successfully

Garlic, a staple in kitchens worldwide, thrives under specific conditions but is generous in its yield when cared for properly. Cultivating garlic successfully involves understanding its growth cycle, soil requirements, and proper planting techniques.

Soil Preparation: Garlic prefers well-drained, fertile soil with a pH of 6.0 to 7.0. Before planting, enrich the soil with organic compost to ensure adequate nutrients. A soil test can guide the amendment process, ensuring the soil is not too acidic or alkaline for optimal growth.

Planting: Garlic is grown from cloves, not seeds. Choose disease-free, large cloves from a reputable nursery or garden center. Planting times vary by climate; in cooler regions, plant cloves in the fall, about four to six weeks before the ground freezes. In warmer climates, garlic may be planted in the late winter or early spring. Plant cloves pointy-end up, 2 inches deep, and 4 to 6 inches apart, in rows spaced 12 to 18 inches apart.

Watering and Mulching: Garlic requires consistent moisture during the growing season, especially in the weeks after planting and during bulb formation. However, it does not tolerate waterlogged soil. Mulching with straw or shredded leaves helps retain soil moisture, suppress weeds, and protect bulbs in colder regions.

Fertilization: Apply a balanced fertilizer at planting time and side-dress with a nitrogen-rich fertilizer in early spring once the garlic begins to grow actively. Avoid high-nitrogen fertilizers close to harvest time, as this can affect bulb development.

Weed Management: Weeds compete with garlic for nutrients and water. Mulching and hand weeding are effective strategies to keep the garlic bed free from competitive weeds without disturbing the garlic roots.

Pest and Disease Control: Garlic has few pests but can be susceptible to onion maggots and fungal diseases like white rot. Crop rotation and proper sanitation, including removing plant debris at the end of the season, are critical in preventing disease buildup.

Harvesting: Garlic is ready to harvest when the lower leaves start to brown and die back, typically in late spring or early summer. Carefully lift the bulbs with a garden fork, avoiding damage. Allow the garlic to cure in a dry, ventilated area for several weeks until the skins are papery.

Storage: After curing, trim the roots and cut the stalks off about 1 inch above the bulb. Store garlic in a cool, dry place with good air circulation. Properly cured garlic can be stored for several months.

Companion Planting: Garlic benefits from being planted near roses and raspberries, deterring pests. However, it should not be planted near peas or beans, as it can inhibit their growth.

In summary, successful garlic cultivation hinges on selecting the proper planting time, preparing the soil with ample organic matter, ensuring proper spacing and depth at planting, regular watering, and diligent weed management. With these technical considerations in mind, gardeners can enjoy a bountiful garlic harvest.

Storage and Preservation Methods for Onions and Garlic

Adequate storage and preservation are crucial for extending the life of onions and garlic, ensuring these culinary staples remain available for use long after harvest. The key to successful storage lies in understanding the conditions each crop requires to maintain freshness and prevent spoilage.

Onion Storage:

- Curing: After harvesting, onions need to be cured to prepare them for storage. Lay them out in a single layer in a dry, well-ventilated area, such as a covered porch or shed, for 2 to 3 weeks. The outer layers should become papery, and the necks should dry out completely.

- Ideal Conditions: Store cured onions in a cool, dry place with temperatures ranging from 35–40°F (2-4°C). Low humidity is essential to prevent mold and rot.

- Ventilation: Use mesh bags or netted sacks to allow air circulation around each onion. Alternatively, onions can be stored in baskets, crates, or hung in braids.

- Location: A basement, garage, or root cellar that meets the temperature and humidity requirements is ideal. Avoid storing onions near potatoes, as the gases released by potatoes can accelerate onions' deterioration.

Garlic Storage:

- Curing: Similar to onions, garlic should be cured after harvesting. Hang the garlic plants or lay them out in a single layer in a dry, well-ventilated area for 2 to 3 weeks until the skins are papery and the roots dry.

- Ideal Conditions: Garlic stores best at room temperature in a dry place with moderate humidity. Temperatures should be maintained around 60–65°F (15–18°C).

- Ventilation: Store garlic in mesh bags, paper bags with holes, or baskets to promote air circulation. Braiding the stems and hanging the braids is also an effective method for soft-neck varieties.

- Avoid Refrigeration: Refrigerating garlic can cause it to sprout prematurely. Keep garlic out of the refrigerator to maintain its dormancy and prolong shelf life.

General Tips for Both Onions and Garlic:

- Inspection: Check stored garlic and onions frequently for deterioration indicators like mold or soft patches. Remove and use any that begin to deteriorate to prevent them from affecting others.

- Usage: Always use onions and garlic from storage that show signs of sprouting or slight softening first, as these are closer to the end of their storage life.

- Variety Matters: Some varieties store better than others. For onions, hard-neck varieties tend to have a longer shelf life than soft-neck varieties. For garlic, soft-neck varieties typically store longer than hard-neck types.

By adhering to these storage and preservation methods, onions and garlic can be kept for several months, reducing waste and ensuring a continuous supply of these essential ingredients.

SEE BONUS APPENDIX 7
THE VARIOUS TYPES OF ONIONS

CHAPTER 9
Eggplant Essentials

Varieties and Planting Tips for Eggplant

Eggplant, known for its versatile use in culinary dishes worldwide, comes in a variety of shapes, sizes, and colors. Understanding the different types of eggplants and the specific conditions they thrive in is essential for a successful harvest.

Varieties of Eggplant:

Globe Eggplant

This is the classic large, purple variety often found in grocery stores. It's excellent for grilling, baking, and frying.

Japanese Eggplant

Longer and thinner than the globe variety, Japanese eggplants have a tender skin and sweet flavor, making them ideal for stir-frying and sautéing.

Italian Eggplant

Slightly smaller than the globe variety, Italian eggplants have a thinner skin and delicate flavor. They are versatile in dishes from pastas to grilled preparations.

White Eggplant

Known for its creamy texture and mild flavor, white eggplant can be used in a variety of dishes, offering a different aesthetic appeal.

Indian Eggplant

Small and round, Indian eggplants are perfect for curries and pickling, known for their rich flavor and easy-to-manage size in cooking.

Planting Tips:

Timing: Eggplants require warm soil and weather to thrive. Plant seeds indoors 6-8 weeks before the last expected frost. Transplant seedlings outdoors when the soil temperature is at least 60°F, typically a few weeks after the last frost when daytime temperatures consistently exceed 70°F.

Soil Preparation: Eggplants prefer rich, well-draining soil with a pH of 5.5 to 6.8. Amend the soil with compost or well-rotted manure to increase fertility. Consider using black plastic mulch to warm the soil and conserve moisture.

Spacing: Plant eggplants 18 to 24 inches apart in rows that are 30 to 36 inches apart. This spacing allows for adequate air circulation and room for growth.

Watering: Keep the soil consistently moist but not waterlogged. Eggplants require 1 to 2 inches of water per week, depending on weather conditions. Drip irrigation or soaker hoses are preferred to keep water off the leaves and prevent disease.

Support: Stake plants early on to support their growth and prevent them from toppling over when laden with fruit.

Mulching: Apply a layer of organic mulch around the plants to help retain soil moisture, regulate soil temperature, and suppress weeds.

Companion Planting: Plant eggplants with green beans, peppers, and thyme to enhance growth and deter pests. Avoid planting near fennel or kohlrabi, which can inhibit eggplant growth.

By selecting the suitable variety for your culinary needs and garden space and following these planting tips, you can enjoy a bountiful harvest of eggplants. Proper care, from soil preparation to spacing and watering, will ensure your eggplants develop fully and provide a versatile ingredient for your kitchen.

Maintenance and Care for Eggplants

Eggplants, with their deep purple hues and versatile culinary uses, are a rewarding addition to any garden. Proper maintenance and care are vital to nurturing healthy plants that yield abundant fruit. Here's a technical guide on caring for eggplants from planting to harvest.

Soil and Site Preparation: Eggplants thrive in well-drained soil rich in organic matter with a pH between 5.5 and 6.8. Before planting, incorporate compost or aged manure into the soil to improve fertility and structure. Select a site that receives at least 6 hours of direct sunlight daily, as eggplants are warmth-loving plants.

Planting: Start eggplant seeds indoors 6-8 weeks before the last frost date. Sow seeds ¼ inch deep in seed-starting mix, maintaining a temperature of 75-85°F for germination. Harden off seedlings gradually before transplanting outdoors when soil temperatures reach at least 60°F, spacing plants 18-24 inches apart in rows 30-36 inches apart.

Watering: Eggplants require consistent moisture for optimal growth, especially during flowering and fruit development. Provide 1 to 2 inches of water per week, adjusting based on rainfall and soil type. Use drip irrigation or soaker hoses to deliver water directly to the root zone, minimizing leaf wetness and disease risk.

Mulching: Apply a 2-3 inches layer of organic mulch around plants to conserve soil moisture, regulate soil temperature, and suppress weeds. Straw, grass clippings, or shredded leaves are suitable materials.

Fertilization: After transplanting, apply a balanced fertilizer, such as a 10-10-10 formula, to encourage strong growth. Once plants begin to flower, side-dress with a high-potassium fertilizer to promote fruit development. Avoid excessive nitrogen, which can lead to lush foliage at the expense of fruiting.

Pest and Disease Management: Common pests include flea beetles, spider mites, and aphids. Manage these through regular monitoring, using insecticidal soaps or neem oil as needed. Crop rotation and proper sanitation help prevent disease. If plants show signs of wilt or leaf spot diseases, remove affected parts and apply appropriate fungicides, following label instructions.

Staking and Support: Provide support to prevent plants from toppling under the weight of the fruit. Use stakes or cages, gently tying the plants to the support structure with soft ties to avoid damage.

Pruning: While not always necessary, removing lower leaves can improve air circulation and reduce disease incidence. Limit pruning to avoid plant stress, focusing on damaged or diseased foliage.

Harvesting: Harvest eggplants when the skin is glossy and the flesh is firm. Use pruning shears to cut the fruit from the plant, leaving a short stem attached. Regular harvesting encourages continued fruit production.

By following these technical guidelines, gardeners can ensure their eggplants receive the care they need to flourish. With diligent maintenance, eggplant plants will produce a generous yield of delicious fruit, ready for culinary use.

Harvesting and Usage of Eggplants

Harvesting eggplants at the right time is crucial for ensuring the best flavor and texture. The timing for harvest depends on the variety and size, but generally, eggplants are ready when the skin becomes shiny and the fruit is firm but slightly under pressure. The color should be deep and uniform. Overripe eggplants may have brown seeds and a bitter taste, while underripe ones will have hard, white seeds and a lackluster flavor.

Techniques for Harvesting:

Use a sharp knife or pruning shears to cut the eggplant from the plant, leaving about an inch of the stem attached. This method prevents damage to the plant and the fruit. Handling eggplants gently is essential as they bruise easily. Frequent harvesting encourages the plant to produce more fruit.

Post-Harvest Care:

After harvesting, store eggplants at room temperature if they will be used within a day or two. For more extended storage, please place them in the crisper drawer of the refrigerator, where they can last for about a week. Avoid washing eggplants before storage, as moisture can lead to decay. Wrap them in a paper towel and place them in a perforated plastic bag to maintain humidity while allowing for some air circulation.

Usage in Culinary Practices:

Eggplants are versatile kitchen ingredients used in a variety of dishes from different cuisines. Before cooking, wash the eggplant under cool running water and trim off the stem. Eggplants can be roasted, grilled, baked, or sautéed and are a staple in dishes such as ratatouille, baba ghanoush, and eggplant parmesan. They can also be diced and added to curries, stir-fries, and salads.

To reduce bitterness, especially in larger or older eggplants, consider salting them before cooking. Cut the eggplant into the desired shape, sprinkle with salt, and let it sit for about 30 minutes. This process draws out some of the bitter-tasting compounds. Rinse the eggplant under cold water and pat dry before cooking.

Nutritional Benefits:

Eggplants are rich in fiber, vitamins, and minerals and are a good source of antioxidants, particularly nigunim, which is found in the skin and may help protect cells from damage. Incorporating eggplants into meals not only adds a rich texture and flavor but also contributes to a healthy, balanced diet.

By following these guidelines for harvesting, storing, and using eggplants, gardeners, and cooks can maximize the enjoyment and benefits of this versatile and nutritious vegetable.

CHAPTER 10
Zucchini and Squash

Planting and Spacing for Zucchini and Squash

When cultivating zucchini and squash, understanding the specific needs for planting and spacing is crucial for healthy growth and abundant production. These warm-season crops thrive in well-drained soil enriched with organic matter and require total sun exposure to develop correctly.

Soil Preparation: Prior to planting, work the soil to a depth of 8-10 inches, incorporating a generous amount of compost or well-rotted manure to provide the necessary nutrients for growth. Ensure the planting site has a pH between 6.0 and 7.0 for optimal nutrient uptake.

Planting Time: Zucchini and squash should be planted after the danger of frost has passed and the soil has warmed to at least 60°F. In most regions, this typically occurs in late spring. For an earlier harvest, seeds can be started indoors 2-3 weeks before the last expected frost date and transplanted outdoors when conditions are suitable.

Sowing Seeds: Seeds should be sown directly into the ground at a depth of 1 inch. For bush varieties, space seeds or seedlings 18-24 inches apart in rows that are 2-3 feet apart. Vining varieties require more space and should be planted 2-3 feet apart in rows that are 4-6 feet apart. If planting in hills, sow 4-6 seeds per hill, with hills spaced 4-6 feet apart for bush types and 6-8 feet apart for vining types. Thin seedlings to 2-3 per hill once they have developed their first true leaves.

Watering: Provide consistent moisture, especially from flowering until harvest. Zucchini and squash need approximately 1-2 inches of water per week. Use drip irrigation or soaker hoses to deliver water directly to the root zone, minimizing leaf wetness and reducing the risk of foliar diseases.

Mulching: Apply a 2-3-inch layer of organic mulch around plants to conserve moisture, regulate soil temperature, and suppress weeds. Straw, grass clippings, or shredded leaves are suitable materials for mulching.

Nutrient Management: Apply a balanced, slow-release fertilizer at planting. Side-dress with a nitrogen-rich fertilizer when the first fruits are about the size of a marble to encourage continued growth and fruit development.

Companion Planting: To enhance growth and deter pests, plant zucchini and squash near companions such as marigolds, which repel nematodes, and nasturtiums, which can prevent squash bugs and beetles. Avoid planting near potatoes, as they can compete for nutrients and attract similar pests.

Pest and Disease Control: Regular monitoring for pests such as squash bugs, cucumber beetles, and vine borers is essential. Employ physical barriers, such as row covers, early in the season to protect plants. Remove and destroy infected plants promptly to prevent the spread of diseases like powdery mildew and bacterial wilt.

By following these technical guidelines for planting and spacing, gardeners can ensure their zucchini and squash plants have the foundation they need for vigorous growth and a prolific harvest. Proper care, including adequate spacing, watering, and nutrient management, will lead to a successful and rewarding growing season.

Managing Pests and Diseases in Zucchini and Squash

Zucchini and squash are susceptible to a variety of pests and diseases that can impact their growth and productivity. Maintaining healthy plants and ensuring a good harvest depend on the application of efficient management techniques.

Pest Management:

Squash Bugs: These pests suck the sap from leaves, causing them to wilt and die. Management includes hand-picking bugs and eggs from the underside of leaves early in the morning and disposing of them in soapy water. Use floating row covers to protect plants, removing them during flowering to allow for pollination.

Cucumber Beetles: These beetles transmit bacterial wilt and can cause significant damage to plants. Use row covers to prevent access to young plants, and remove any wilted plants promptly to reduce disease spread. Apply insecticidal soap or neem oil as needed, following product instructions.

Squash Vine Borers: These larvae bore into squash stems, causing plants to wilt suddenly. Wrap the base of the stems with aluminum foil to prevent egg-laying, and monitor plants for signs of borer activity. If borers are detected, carefully slit the stem and remove the borer, then cover the damaged area with soil to encourage rooting.

Disease Management:

Powdery Mildew: This fungal disease appears as white, powdery spots on leaves and stems. Increase air circulation by spacing plants properly and pruning any overcrowded areas. Apply a mixture of baking soda and water or use a sulfur-based fungicide to control outbreaks.

Bacterial Wilt: Spread by cucumber beetles, this disease causes plants to wilt and die rapidly. Control cucumber beetles and remove any infected plants immediately to prevent the spread of the disease.

Downy Mildew: Downy mildew is a plant that grows best in damp environments. It is identified by yellow spots on the upper surface of leaves and fuzzy growth on the underside. To manage, water plants at the base to keep foliage dry and apply copper-based fungicides at the first sign of the disease.

Preventative Measures:

Crop Rotation: Avoid planting zucchini and squash in the same location year after year to reduce the buildup of pests and diseases in the soil.

Sanitation: Keep the garden area clean of plant debris and weeds, which can harbor pests and diseases.

Healthy Soil: Maintain soil health with regular applications of compost and organic matter to support vigorous plant growth.

Resistant Varieties: Whenever possible, choose disease-resistant varieties of zucchini and squash to reduce the need for chemical interventions.

Companion Planting:

Planting zucchini and squash with companion plants like marigolds, nasturtiums, and tansies can help deter pests naturally. Marigolds repel nematodes and other soil pests, while nasturtiums can attract aphids away from squash plants.

By implementing these technical strategies for pest and disease management, gardeners can protect their zucchini and squash plants, ensuring a bountiful and healthy harvest. Regular monitoring and prompt action at the first sign of problems are crucial to maintaining plant health throughout the growing season.

Harvesting and Storage of Zucchini and Squash

Harvesting zucchini and squash at the optimal time ensures the best flavor and texture for both immediate use and storage. These vegetables are generally easy to grow and prolific producers, making timely harvesting essential to avoid overly large, seedy, and less flavorful fruits.

Harvesting Techniques:

Timing: Zucchini should be harvested when they are about 6-8 inches long. Squash varieties have different optimal sizes, but most summer squashes are best when harvested at a similar size to zucchini. Winter squash, such as butternut and acorn, should be harvested when the rind is hard and they have reached their mature color.

Method: Use a sharp knife or pruning shears to cut the fruit from the plant, leaving a small piece of stem attached. This helps to prolong the vegetable's shelf life by preventing moisture loss and decay at the cut site.

Frequency: Check plants every other day during the growing season, as zucchini and squash can proliferate. Regular harvesting encourages the plant to produce more fruit.

Storage Techniques:

Summer Squash (including Zucchini): These are best used fresh but can be stored in the refrigerator for up to 1 week. Place them in a perforated plastic bag to allow for some air circulation. For more extended storage, summer squash can be sliced and blanched for 3 minutes, then cooled, drained, and packed into freezer bags for freezing.

Winter Squash: Cure winter squash (except for acorn squash, which does not require curing) by storing them in a warm, dry place (about 80°F) for 10 days to 2 weeks. After curing, move them to a cool, dry place where temperatures are between 50-55°F for storage. Properly cured winter squash can last for several months under these conditions.

Preparation for Storage: Clean the surface of winter squash with a weak bleach solution (1 part bleach to 10 parts water) to kill surface bacteria and fungi. Dry them thoroughly before storing them to prevent rot.

Usage:

Summer Squash: These are versatile in the kitchen, used in dishes ranging from sautéed sides to bread and casseroles. They can be eaten raw, cooked, or grated and frozen for future use in baking.

Winter Squash: These are typically used in soups, baked dishes, and purees. The flesh can be roasted, steamed, or boiled. Squash can also be cut into pieces and frozen, or the pureed flesh can be stored in freezer bags.

Companion Planting for Enhanced Production:

Planting zucchini and squash near flowers like marigolds can deter pests. Companion planting with corn and beans, known as the "Three Sisters," provides mutual benefits: the squash leaves shade the soil, helping to retain moisture and suppress weeds, while the beans add nitrogen to the soil, benefiting all three crops.

By following these guidelines for harvesting and storage, gardeners can enjoy the fruits of their labor for as long as possible, ensuring a steady supply of zucchini and squash for both immediate consumption and future culinary creations.

CHAPTER 11
Cabbage Family Wonders

Growing Different Types of Cabbage

Cabbage, a versatile and nutritious vegetable, belongs to the Brassica family and comes in various types, each with its unique characteristics and growing requirements. Understanding these can help gardeners achieve a bountiful harvest.

Green Cabbage

The most common variety, green cabbage, has tight, compact heads and a slightly peppery flavor. It's hardy and can be planted early in the spring. For a fall harvest, plant mid-summer. Space plants 12-24 inches apart in rows, allowing 24-36 inches between rows. Green cabbage requires full sun, consistent moisture, and rich, well-drained soil with plenty of organic matter.

Red Cabbage

Known for its vibrant color and slightly sweet taste, red cabbage thrives under similar conditions to green cabbage but may take a bit longer to mature. It benefits from the same planting distances as green cabbage. Red cabbage's color intensifies and flavor improves with cooler temperatures, making it an excellent choice for fall harvesting.

Savoy Cabbage

Savoy cabbage, characterized by its crinkled leaves and mild flavor, prefers cooler growing conditions. Plant it in early spring or late summer for a fall harvest, using the same spacing as green and red cabbage. Savoy cabbage is less dense, making it more susceptible to pests; thus, integrated pest management practices are essential.

Napa Cabbage

Also known as Chinese cabbage, Napa cabbage has oblong heads and crinkly, pale green leaves. It prefers cooler weather and should be planted in late summer for a fall harvest. Space plants 12-15 inches apart in rows that are 18-30 inches apart. Napa cabbage requires consistent watering and fertile soil to develop its full flavor and texture.

Bok Choy

A type of Chinese cabbage that does not form heads, Bok Choy is grown for its tender leaves and stalks. It can be harvested young for baby greens or left to mature. Plant in early spring or late summer, spacing plants 6-12 inches apart in rows 18-30 inches apart. Bok Choy prefers cooler temperatures and can bolt if planted too late in spring.

Care Tips for All Types:

Watering: Provide at least 1 inch of water per week, more during hot, dry periods. Mulching helps retain soil moisture and keeps roots cool.

Fertilization: Apply a balanced fertilizer at planting and a nitrogen-rich fertilizer mid-season to support leafy growth.

Pest Management: Common pests include cabbage loopers, aphids, and flea beetles. To protect young plants, organic pesticides must be applied as necessary.

Disease Prevention: Practice crop rotation and provide adequate spacing for air circulation to reduce the risk of diseases like black rot and clubroot.

Companion Planting: Planting cabbage near aromatic herbs like dill, rosemary, and mint can help repel certain pests. Avoid planting near strawberries, tomatoes, and pole beans, as they can inhibit cabbage's growth.

By catering to the specific needs of each cabbage type, from soil preparation and spacing to pest and disease management, gardeners can enjoy a diverse and successful cabbage crop, ready for culinary use in salads, sautéed dishes, and fermentations.

Dealing with Common Cabbage Pests

The cultivation of cabbage and its relatives often invites a host of common pests, each capable of inflicting significant damage if not promptly managed. Understanding these pests and implementing effective control strategies is crucial for maintaining healthy cabbage family crops.

Cabbage Loopers and Worms: These caterpillars are known for their voracious appetite, feeding on leaves and creating irregular holes. To manage these pests, monitor plants regularly and remove caterpillars by hand when spotted. Applying Bacillus thuringiensis (Bt), a naturally occurring bacterium, can effectively control these larvae without harming beneficial insects.

Aphids: Small, soft-bodied insects that cluster on the undersides of leaves; aphids suck plant sap, causing leaves to curl and weaken. They also excrete a sticky substance called honeydew, which can lead to sooty mold. Control aphids by spraying plants with a strong jet of water to knock them off or by using insecticidal soap or neem oil as a targeted treatment.

Flea Beetles: These small, jumping beetles chew tiny holes in leaves, which can severely impact young plants. To deter flea beetles, use floating row covers to protect plants, especially during seedling stages. Diatomaceous earth or pyrethrin-based insecticides can also be applied to infested plants.

Cabbage Root Maggots: The larvae of a fly that targets the roots of cabbage family plants, causing wilting and stunted growth. Prevention is critical; protective collars should be placed around the base of seedlings at planting time to prevent adults from laying eggs near the plants. Crop rotation and proper sanitation, as well as removing plant debris and weeds, can help break the life cycle of these pests.

Harlequin Bugs: Shield-shaped bugs that feed on plant sap, leading to spotted and wilted leaves. Handpick bugs and eggs or use floating row covers to prevent infestation. In severe cases, insecticidal soap or neem oil may be used, focusing applications on the undersides of leaves where bugs congregate.

Preventive Strategies:

- Healthy Soil: Maintaining rich, well-drained soil helps plants resist pests and diseases.

- Companion Planting: Growing aromatic herbs like thyme, rosemary, and mint near cabbage can deter many pests. Marigolds can repel cabbage moths and nematodes.

- Biological Control: Introducing beneficial insects, such as ladybugs and lacewings, can help naturally reduce aphid populations.

- Crop Rotation: To reduce soil-borne pests and diseases, avoid planting cabbage family crops in the same location year after year.

Monitoring and Early Intervention: Regular inspection of plants allows for the early detection of pests, which is crucial for effective management. Implementing a combination of physical, biological, and, when necessary, chemical controls can maintain a balanced ecosystem in your garden, minimizing the impact of pests on cabbage family crops.

By adhering to these technical strategies, gardeners can effectively manage common pests, ensuring the health and productivity of their cabbage family plants.

Harvesting and Culinary Uses of Cabbage Family Plants

Harvesting cabbage family plants at the optimal time ensures peak flavor and nutritional value, setting the stage for a variety of culinary uses. This diverse family, including cabbage, broccoli, kale, and Brussels sprouts, offers a wealth of options for garden-to-table dishes.

Harvesting Techniques:

- Cabbage: Harvest when heads are firm and have reached the desired size, typically between 7 and 9 inches in diameter. Use a sharp knife to cut the head from the base of the plant, leaving a few outer leaves to protect it.

- Broccoli: For best taste, harvest broccoli while the flower buds are still tight and before yellow petals start to emerge. Cut the central head off with a sharp knife, leaving about 6 inches of stem to encourage the growth of side shoots.

- Kale: Harvest young leaves for the best flavor, cutting them from the outer edges of the plant. Kale is a cut-and-come-again vegetable; new growth will continue to emerge from the center.

- Brussels Sprouts: Harvest from the bottom of the stalk when sprouts are firm, green, and about 1 inch in diameter. Twist them off by hand or cut them with a knife.

Culinary Uses:

- Cabbage: Can be used raw in salads and slaws or cooked in dishes such as soups, stews, and stuffed cabbage rolls. Fermented cabbage, known as sauerkraut or kimchi, is a probiotic-rich food.

- Broccoli: Versatile in both raw and cooked forms, broccoli can be steamed, roasted, stir-fried, or added to soups and casseroles. The stems and leaves are also edible and nutritious.

- Kale: A nutrient-dense leafy green, kale can be used in salads, smoothies, and chips. It's also excellent sautéed with garlic or added to soups for a hearty texture.

- Brussels Sprouts: They are best roasted, steamed, or sautéed. They can be seasoned with olive oil, salt, and pepper or glazed with balsamic vinegar for a caramelized finish.

Storage Tips:

- Cabbage and Brussels Sprouts: Store in the refrigerator in a plastic bag for up to several weeks. They keep best when cool and slightly humid.

- Broccoli: Keep in the refrigerator in a loose, perforated plastic bag for up to a week. Do not wash before storing to avoid moisture buildup.

- Kale: Store in the refrigerator in a plastic bag with a damp paper towel to keep the leaves moist. For best quality, use within 5-7 days.

Companion Planting for Flavor Enhancement:

Planting cabbage family crops near herbs such as dill, mint, and rosemary can enhance their flavor and deter pests. Additionally, growing onions or garlic nearby can help repel common pests like aphids and cabbage loopers.

By understanding the specific harvesting indicators and storage requirements of each cabbage family plant, gardeners can maximize their garden's yield and enjoy a variety of nutritious, flavorful dishes throughout the season.

CHAPTER 12
Peppers: From Sweet to Heat

Selecting Varieties and Starting Seeds for Peppers

The journey to cultivating peppers, ranging from sweet bell peppers to fiery habaneros, begins with the careful selection of varieties and the proper starting of seeds. This process is both an art and a science, requiring an understanding of your garden's specific conditions and a strategy for seed germination that sets the stage for a successful growing season.

Variety Selection: The first step in growing peppers is selecting the suitable varieties to match your climate, taste preferences, and culinary uses. Peppers vary widely in flavor, heat, and growth habits:

Sweet Peppers

Include bell peppers of various colors and sweet non-bell types like banana and pimento. Ideal for fresh eating, roasting, and stuffing.

Hot Peppers

They range from moderately spicy jalapeños and serranoes to extremely hot varieties like ghost peppers and Carolina reapers. Choose based on your heat tolerance and intended use in cooking.

Heirloom Varieties

They offer unique flavors and colors not found in standard types. They can be more susceptible to pests and diseases, but they are often more flavorful.

Hybrid Varieties

Bred for disease resistance, yield, and uniformity. It is ideal for gardeners looking for reliability and specific traits.

Starting Seeds Indoors: Peppers require a long, warm growing season, so starting seeds indoors is often necessary, especially in cooler climates.

- Timing: Start pepper seeds indoors 8-10 weeks before the last expected frost date. This gives plants a head start, ensuring they mature and produce fruit within the growing season.

- Soil and Containers: Use a sterile, seed-starting mix in small pots or trays. Ensure containers have drainage holes to prevent waterlogged soil.

- Planting: Plant seeds ¼ inch deep. Keep the soil moist but not waterlogged, and maintain a temperature of 70-85°F for optimal germination. A heat mat can help maintain a consistent soil temperature.

- Lighting: Once seeds germinate, provide 14-16 hours of light daily using grow lights or a sunny windowsill. Proper light prevents seedlings from becoming leggy.

- Transplanting: Harden off seedlings by gradually introducing them to outdoor conditions over a week. Transplant outdoors after all danger of frost has passed and nighttime temperatures consistently stay above 55°F.

Seedling Care:

- Watering: Keep the soil consistently moist but not saturated. Overwatering can lead to damping-off, a fatal seedling disease.

- Fertilizing: Once seedlings develop their second set of true leaves, begin feeding with a half-strength, water-soluble fertilizer every two weeks.

- Thinning: If starting in trays, thin seedlings to prevent overcrowding, allowing the strongest to continue growing.

By selecting the right pepper varieties for your garden and following best practices for starting seeds indoors, you can ensure a robust start to your pepper plants. This foundational step is critical for developing vigorous, productive plants that will yield an abundant harvest of peppers, from the sweetest bells to the hottest chilies.

Soil Preparation and Optimal Conditions for Peppers

Peppers, whether sweet or spicy, demand specific soil conditions and environmental factors to flourish. Preparing the garden bed meticulously and ensuring the optimal growing conditions are met can significantly influence the health of the plants and the quality of the pepper harvest. Here's a technical guide to setting the stage for a successful pepper crop.

Soil Preparation: The foundation of vibrant pepper plants begins with the soil. Peppers thrive in well-drained, loamy soil with a pH range of 6.0 to 6.8. To prepare the bed:

- Testing: Conduct a soil test to determine the pH and nutrient levels. Based on the test results, amend the soil to balance the pH and enrich it with necessary nutrients.

- Organic Matter: Incorporate a generous amount of organic matter, such as compost or well-rotted manure, into the soil before planting. This improves soil structure, enhances moisture retention, and provides a slow-release source of nutrients.

- Drainage: Ensure adequate drainage at the planting location to avoid soggy conditions that might cause root infections. Raised beds or ridges can improve drainage for peppers.

Optimal Conditions:

- Sunlight: Peppers require full sun, at least 6 to 8 hours of direct sunlight per day. Choose a planting site that receives ample sunlight to promote vigorous growth and fruit development.

- Temperature: Peppers are warm-season crops that germinate and grow best at temperatures between 70°F and 85°F. Planting should occur after the last frost when soil temperatures reach at least 60°F. If necessary, use black plastic mulch to warm the soil.

- Spacing: Proper spacing is crucial to allow for adequate air circulation and reduce disease pressure. Space pepper plants 18 to 24 inches apart in rows that are 24 to 36 inches apart. This spacing varies slightly depending on the variety and its growth habit.

Water and Mulch:

- Watering: Consistent moisture is critical to preventing stress and encouraging steady growth. Peppers need about 1 to 2 inches of water per week, depending on weather conditions. The best way to provide water to the root zone without wetting the foliage is by drip irrigation.

- Mulching: Apply a 2-3 inches layer of organic mulch around pepper plants to conserve soil moisture, moderate soil temperature, and suppress weeds. Straw, grass clippings, or shredded leaves are practical mulches for pepper plants.

Soil Health Maintenance:

- Crop Rotation: To reduce the risk of soil-borne diseases, avoid planting peppers in the same location where tomatoes, potatoes, or other members of the Solanaceae family have grown in the past three years.

- Nutrient Management: Side-dress pepper plants with a balanced fertilizer or compost during the growing season to support vigorous growth and fruiting. Be cautious not to over-fertilize, as excessive nitrogen can lead to lush foliage at the expense of fruit production.

By diligently preparing the soil and creating the optimal conditions, gardeners can cultivate healthy pepper plants capable of producing an abundant harvest. Attention to detail in these early stages lays the groundwork for a season of gardening success, yielding a colorful and flavorful pepper crop.

Planting, Watering, and Fertilization Techniques for Peppers

Mastering the cultivation of peppers, from the sweetest bell to the fieriest chili, requires a nuanced approach to planting, watering, and fertilization. These techniques are pivotal to nurturing robust plants capable of yielding a bountiful harvest. Here's a detailed guide to optimizing these practices for pepper plants.

Planting Techniques:

- Timing: Transplant pepper seedlings outdoors once the threat of frost has passed and soil temperatures consistently exceed 60°F. Peppers are warm-season crops that thrive in heat.

- Soil Preparation: Ensure the garden bed is well-tilled, incorporating ample organic matter to promote drainage and fertility. Peppers flourish in loamy, nutrient-rich soil.

- Spacing: Allow 18-24 inches between each plant and 24-36 inches between rows. This spacing accommodates the mature size of the plants and facilitates air circulation, reducing the risk of fungal diseases.

- Depth: Plant seedlings at the same depth they were growing in their containers to prevent stem rot. Firm the soil gently around the base and water immediately to settle the soil.

Watering Practices:

- Consistency: Peppers demand consistent moisture for optimal growth, particularly during flowering and fruit set. Provide 1-2 inches of water per week, adjusting for rainfall to avoid over-saturation.

- Method: Utilize drip irrigation or soaker hoses to deliver water directly to the root zone, minimizing moisture on leaves and thus reducing the likelihood of leaf diseases.

- Mulching: Apply a 2-3 inches layer of organic mulch around plants to retain soil moisture, regulate soil temperature, and suppress weed growth.

Fertilization Strategy:

- Initial Application: Incorporate a balanced, slow-release fertilizer into the soil at planting time to provide a steady supply of nutrients. Peppers benefit from a fertilizer ratio close to 5-10-10 (N-P-K).

- Growth Phase: Once the first fruits begin to form, side-dress with a low-nitrogen, high-phosphorus fertilizer to encourage fruit development over foliage. Too much nitrogen can result in lush leaves at the expense of fruit.

- Calcium: Peppers are susceptible to blossom end rot, a calcium deficiency disorder. Ensure adequate calcium levels in the soil by adding amendments or using calcium-containing fertilizers.

Additional Considerations:

- pH Level: Maintain a soil pH between 6.0 and 6.8. Adjust soil pH accordingly based on soil test results, using lime to raise the pH or sulfur to lower it.

- Support: Provide support for pepper plants with stakes or cages to keep burgeoning fruit off the ground, reducing disease exposure and pest attacks.
- Companion Planting: Grow peppers alongside compatible plants like basil, which can repel certain pests and potentially enhance the flavor of the peppers.

By adhering to these precise planting, watering, and fertilization techniques, gardeners can foster the growth of vigorous pepper plants. These practices lay the groundwork for a productive season, culminating in the harvest of crisp, flavorful peppers that are a testament to the gardener's skill and dedication.

Battling Pests and Diseases in Peppers

Growing peppers, from the crispest bell to the fiercest habanero, presents a myriad of challenges, notably in the form of pests and diseases. These adversaries can significantly impact plant health and yield if not managed promptly and effectively. Herein lies a technical guide to identifying, preventing, and controlling common pests and diseases that afflict pepper plants.

Pest Management:

1. Aphids: These tiny pests congregate on the undersides of leaves, sucking sap and excreting sticky honeydew. Control aphids by blasting them off with water or applying insecticidal soap. Introduce beneficial insects, such as ladybugs, that feed on aphids.

2. Spider Mites: Indicated by fine webbing and discolored leaves, spider mites thrive in hot, dry conditions. Increase humidity around plants and use miticides or neem oil as a control measure.

3. Cutworms: These nocturnal caterpillars cut young plants at the soil line. Wrap a collar around the plant's base and maintain a clean garden to deter them.

4. Pepper Weevils: A more specialized pest, pepper weevils bore into fruits, causing them to drop prematurely. Remove and destroy infested fruits and practice crop rotation.

Disease Control:

1. Bacterial Spot: Manifesting as small, water-soaked spots on leaves and fruits, this disease can devastate crops. Use copper-based fungicides and ensure plants are spaced to improve air circulation.

2. Powdery Mildew: Identified by a powdery white coating on leaves, powdery mildew is combated with sulfur or milk sprays. Ensure plants receive adequate sunlight and air movement.

3. Fusarium and Verticillium Wilts: These soil-borne fungal diseases cause wilting and yellowing of leaves. Select resistant varieties and practice soil solarization to reduce fungal spores.

Preventive Measures:

- Crop Rotation: Avoid planting peppers in the same spot year after year to minimize disease carryover.

- Sanitation: Keep the area around plants free from debris and weeds that can harbor pests and diseases.

- Proper Watering: Water plants at the soil level to avoid wetting foliage, which can lead to fungal diseases. Drip irrigation is ideal for this.

- Healthy Soil: Amend soil with compost to improve its structure, fertility, and microbial activity, making plants more resilient to pests and diseases.

- Barrier Methods: Use floating row covers to protect plants from early-season pests. Remove covers when plants flower to allow for pollination.

By implementing these strategies, gardeners can significantly reduce the impact of pests and diseases on their pepper crops. Vigilance, combined with an integrated approach to pest and disease management, ensures that interventions are timely and effective, preserving the health of the plants and the abundance of the harvest.

Harvesting and Utilizing Peppers

The culmination of cultivating peppers, from the tender sweetness of bell peppers to the scorching zest of ghost peppers, is the harvest and subsequent utilization of these versatile fruits. The process of harvesting peppers at the right time and using them in a variety of culinary applications is as much an art as it is a science. This section delves into the techniques for harvesting peppers at their peak and suggestions for their use in the kitchen.

Harvesting Techniques:

- Timing: The ideal time to harvest peppers depends on the variety and desired maturity. Sweet peppers are usually harvested when they reach full size and are vividly colored. Hot peppers may be picked when they are green for a milder flavor or allowed to mature to red for maximum heat.

- Method: Use a sharp pair of scissors or pruning shears to cut the pepper from the plant, leaving a short stub of stem attached. This method minimizes damage to the plant and the fruit, reducing the chance of rot or infection.

- Signs of Readiness: Look for firm, glossy fruits that are uniform in color. The skin should be taught and the flesh firm to the touch. For hot peppers, the presence of small, fine lines or wrinkles near the stem can indicate peak ripeness and heat.

Utilization in the Kitchen:

- Fresh Consumption: Both sweet and hot peppers can be eaten fresh. Slice them into salads, sandwiches, or salsas for a crisp, flavorful addition. Sweet peppers can also be stuffed with rice, meat, or cheese mixtures and baked.

- Cooking: Peppers of all types can be roasted, grilled, sautéed, or added to stir-fries and casseroles. Cooking can enhance the sweetness of bell peppers and temper the heat of spicier varieties.

- Preservation: Peppers lend themselves well to preservation methods. Sweet peppers can be canned or pickled, while hot peppers are ideal for drying or making into powders, sauces, and salsas. Freezing is another option for both sweet and hot peppers; slice or chop them before freezing for easier use later.

- Infusing Oils and Vinegar: Hot peppers can be used to infuse oils and vinegar, creating flavorful condiments for cooking or dressing salads.

Special Considerations:

- Handling Hot Peppers: When processing hot peppers, wear gloves to protect your skin from capsaicin, the compound that gives peppers their heat. Avoid touching your face or eyes.

- Seed Saving: For those interested in saving seeds, choose mature peppers from healthy, non-hybrid plants. Clean and dry the seeds before storing them in a cool, dry place for the next planting season.

By following these harvesting and utilization techniques, gardeners can maximize the yield and flavor of their pepper crops. Whether incorporating fresh peppers into daily meals or preserving them for future use, the versatility of peppers makes them a rewarding crop for any gardener.

CHAPTER 13
Pest Control in the Garden

Identifying Common Garden Pests

Effective pest management in the garden begins with accurate identification of the culprits. Familiarizing oneself with the characteristics and behaviors of common garden pests is the first step towards maintaining plant health and ensuring bountiful harvests. Here's a technical overview of several pervasive pests and how to identify them.

Aphids
Small, soft-bodied insects that can be green, black, brown, or pink, aphids cluster on the undersides of leaves and tender shoot tips, sucking plant sap and excreting a sticky substance known as honeydew. Infestations can lead to distorted growth and sooty mold.

Spider Mites
Tiny spider-like pests, often red or brown, live on the undersides of leaves, creating delicate webs. They pierce plant cells to feed, causing yellowing or bronzing of leaves and, in severe cases, leaf drop.

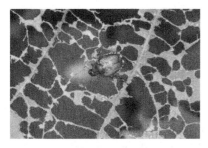

Japanese Beetles
Metallic blue-green beetles, about ½ inch long, with bronze wing covers. They feed on a wide range of plants, chewing leaves and flowers, often leaving a skeletonized pattern.

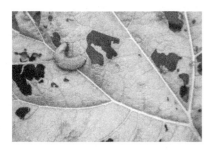

Slugs and Snails
Soft-bodied mollusks that feed at night, leaving a slimy trail. They create irregular holes with smooth edges in leaves, flowers, and tender plant stems.

Cabbage Loopers and Worms
Caterpillars that target members of the cabbage family, chewing large, ragged holes in leaves. Loopers are light green with a white stripe on each side, moving with a distinctive "looping" motion.

Squash Vine Borers
Larvae of a moth that bore into the stems of squash plants, causing wilting. They are white with a dark head and can be found inside the stem near the base of the plant.

Cutworms
Gray or brown caterpillars that curl into a C-shape when disturbed. They feed at night, cutting off young plants at the soil line or feeding on lower leaves.

Flea Beetles
Small, dark beetles that jump like fleas when disturbed. They chew tiny holes in leaves, especially favoring young plants, which can stunt growth or even kill the seedlings.

Tomato Hornworms
Large, green caterpillars with white and black markings and a distinctive horn on their rear. They feed on tomato, pepper, eggplant, and potato plants and quickly defoliate them.

Whiteflies
Tiny, white-winged insects that congregate in clouds around infected plants. They feed on plant sap, weakening the host and potentially transmitting diseases.

Management Techniques: Once identified, garden pests can often be managed through a combination of cultural, physical, and biological methods. Regular monitoring, proper plant care, and the introduction of natural predators can significantly reduce pest populations. In cases where intervention is necessary, organic and least-toxic options should be explored first to minimize environmental impact and preserve beneficial insect populations.

Understanding the habits and identifying features of these common pests empowers gardeners to take early action, often preventing minor issues from becoming major infestations.

Organic Pest Control Methods

In the pursuit of maintaining a healthy and productive garden, organic pest control methods offer a sustainable approach to managing garden pests. These methods prioritize ecological balance and soil health, employing strategies that minimize harm to beneficial insects and the environment. Here's a technical overview of effective organic pest control techniques.

Physical Barriers and Traps:

- Floating Row Covers: Lightweight fabric draped over plants can protect them from a variety of pests, including aphids, beetles, and moths, while still allowing light and water to penetrate.

- Sticky Traps: Colored sticky cards can attract and trap flying insects like whiteflies and aphids. Yellow traps are particularly effective.

- Hand Picking: Manually removing pests such as caterpillars, slugs, and snails early in the morning or late evening can significantly reduce populations.

Biological Controls:

- Beneficial Insects: Introducing or encouraging beneficial insects that prey on pests is a cornerstone of organic pest management. Ladybugs, lacewings, and predatory mites feed on aphids, mites, and other harmful insects.

- Nematodes: Soil-dwelling beneficial nematodes can control soil-borne pests like grubs and root weevils by infecting and killing them without harming plants.

- Bacillus thuringiensis (Bt): A naturally occurring bacterium used as a selective insecticide, Bt is ingested by caterpillars and certain other pests, causing them to stop feeding and die.

Cultural Practices:

- Crop Rotation: Rotating crops annually helps prevent the buildup of pests and diseases associated with specific plant families.

- Sanitation: Regularly removing plant debris and weeds from the garden eliminates breeding grounds and overwintering sites for pests.

- Companion Planting: Growing certain plants together can deter pests. For example, marigolds emit a substance that repels nematodes and other pests, while garlic and onions can deter beetles and aphids.

Organic Sprays and Treatments:

- Insecticidal Soaps and Oils: Products based on potassium salts of fatty acids (insecticidal soap) and neem oil can safely control many soft-bodied pests on contact without harming beneficial insects.

- Diatomaceous Earth: A powder made from crushed fossilized algae, diatomaceous earth can be sprinkled around the base of plants to deter and physically damage crawling pests like slugs and cutworms.

- Homemade Sprays: Solutions made from everyday household items, such as garlic, chili peppers, or vinegar, can provide temporary pest deterrence. Always test a small area of the plant first to ensure it is not harmful.

Soil Health:

- Maintaining rich, well-drained soil through the addition of organic matter and compost supports strong plant growth, making them less susceptible to pests and diseases.

Implementing these organic pest control methods requires patience and persistence but contributes to a more resilient garden ecosystem. By focusing on prevention, encouraging natural predators, and using non-toxic treatments judiciously, gardeners can effectively manage pests while safeguarding the environment.

Preventive Strategies in Garden Pest Control

Effective garden management encompasses proactive measures designed to prevent pest infestations before they begin. These strategies, grounded in the principles of integrated pest management (IPM), aim to create an environment less hospitable to pests while promoting healthy growth in plants. Here's a detailed overview of preventive strategies for garden pest control.

Soil Health: Maintaining robust soil health is foundational. Rich, well-aerated soil fortified with organic matter supports vigorous plant growth, making plants less susceptible to pest attacks. Regular amendments with compost or well-rotted manure enhance soil fertility and structure, providing plants with the nutrients needed to withstand pest pressure.

Cultural Practices:

- Crop Rotation: Rotating crops each year reduces the buildup of pest populations by interrupting their life cycles. Different plant families should not be planted in the same location more frequently than once every three years.

- Sanitation: Keeping the garden clean by removing plant debris, fallen fruits, and weeds eliminates potential breeding grounds and overwintering sites for pests.

- Water Management: Proper irrigation techniques, such as drip irrigation or soaker hoses, apply water directly to the soil, keeping foliage dry and less prone to pest invasions.

Physical Barriers:

- Row Covers: Floating row covers made of lightweight fabric can be placed over crops to physically block pests while still allowing light, air, and moisture to reach the plants.

- Mulching: A layer of organic mulch can prevent soil-dwelling pests from reaching plant bases and discourage some pests by creating a barrier they are unwilling to cross.

- Netting and Fencing: Installing netting or fencing can deter larger pests like birds and mammals from accessing plants.

Plant Selection:

- Resistant Varieties: Opting for plant varieties known for their resistance to specific pests can significantly reduce pest issues.

- Diverse Plantings: Incorporating a diversity of plants within the garden can reduce pest outbreaks by disrupting the monoculture environment in which many pests thrive.

Companion Planting: Strategically planting certain crops together can repel pests or attract beneficial insects. For example, planting marigolds can deter nematodes, while basil may repel flies and mosquitoes.

Timing: Adjusting planting times can help avoid peak pest populations. For instance, planting earlier or later than usual can allow crops to mature during periods when pests are less active.

Beneficial Insects: Encouraging or introducing beneficial insects that prey on pest species is a natural way to control pest populations. Practices such as planting pollinator-friendly flowers or creating habitats for predatory insects can enhance the presence of these natural allies.

Monitoring: Regularly inspecting plants for signs of pests allows for early detection and intervention, preventing minor issues from escalating into significant infestations.

By integrating these preventive strategies into garden practices, gardeners can effectively manage pest populations, reducing the need for reactive measures. This approach not only promotes a more sustainable gardening ecosystem but also supports the long-term health and productivity of the garden.

CHAPTER 14

Disease Management

Common Plant Diseases

In the realm of gardening, disease management is a crucial aspect of ensuring plant health and maximizing yields. A variety of pathogens can afflict garden plants, leading to a range of symptoms and potential crop loss. Understanding these common diseases is the first step toward effective management and prevention. Here's a detailed look at some prevalent plant diseases, their symptoms, and the conditions they thrive in.

Powdery Mildew:

- <u>Symptoms</u>: A white, powdery fungal growth on leaf surfaces, stems, and sometimes flowers or fruit.
- <u>Conditions</u>: Thrives in warm, dry climates with cool nights. Overcrowding and poor air circulation contribute to its spread.
- <u>Impact</u>: Hinders photosynthesis, weakening plants and diminishing yields.

Downy Mildew:

- <u>Symptoms</u>: Yellow patches on upper leaf surfaces with a fluffy, grayish-white fungal growth on the undersides.
- <u>Conditions</u>: Prefers cool, wet weather. It often occurs in spring and fall.
- <u>Impact</u>: Can lead to leaf drop, stunted growth, and reduced fruit quality.

Rust:

- <u>Symptoms</u>: Small, rust-colored pustules on the undersides of leaves, which may turn yellow and drop.
- <u>Conditions</u>: Favored by warm, moist conditions. Spores are windborne and can infect plants from a distance.
- <u>Impact</u>: Reduces plant vigor and, in severe cases, can lead to plant death.

Fusarium and Verticillium Wilts:

- Symptoms: Yellowing and wilting of leaves, starting at the base of the plant. Stems may show a brown discoloration inside.
- Conditions: Soil-borne fungi that persist in the soil for years. Warm temperatures for Fusarium and cooler temperatures for Verticillium favor disease development.
- Impact: Can kill plants outright or severely limit their productivity.

Root Rot:

- Symptoms: Rotted, mushy roots accompanied by wilting, yellowing, and stunted growth above ground.
- Conditions: Overwatering and poor drainage create an ideal environment for fungal pathogens.
- Impact: Often fatal if not addressed early, as the plant's ability to take up water and nutrients is compromised.

Bacterial Spot and Canker:

- Symptoms: Dark, water-soaked spots on leaves, stems, and fruit. Cankers may form on stems.
- Conditions: Spread by water splash and infected tools. Warm, wet weather exacerbates the issue.
- Impact: Reduces yield and can cause premature fruit drop.

Management Strategies: Effective disease management integrates several practices:

- Cultural Controls: Implement crop rotation, proper spacing, and sanitation to reduce pathogen sources.

- Resistant Varieties: Select plant varieties bred for resistance to specific diseases.

- Environmental Controls: Adjust watering practices and improve soil drainage to discourage pathogen growth.

- Organic Fungicides: Apply copper or sulfur-based fungicides as preventive measures during susceptible periods.

By familiarizing themselves with these common diseases and implementing strategic management practices, gardeners can significantly reduce the impact of pathogens on their gardens. The secret to keeping plants healthy and fruitful is to be vigilant and take preventative action.

Organic Treatment Options for Plant Diseases

In the pursuit of sustainable gardening, managing plant diseases with organic methods is both a practical and environmentally friendly approach. Organic disease management focuses on using non-synthetic products and practices to control or eliminate pathogens while preserving soil health, beneficial organisms, and the surrounding ecosystem. Here, we explore a variety of organic treatment options that can be effectively integrated into a comprehensive disease management strategy.

Biological Fungicides:

- Bacillus subtilis: A beneficial bacterium that colonizes plant roots and leaves, producing substances antagonistic to various fungal pathogens. It's effective against powdery mildew, gray mold, and leaf spots.

- Trichoderma harzianum: A fungus that outcompetes harmful pathogens for space and nutrients. It's particularly useful for soil-borne diseases like root rot and damping-off.

Botanical Extracts and Oils:

- Neem Oil: Derived from the seeds of the neem tree, it offers a broad spectrum of action against fungal diseases, including rust, scab, and blight. It also deters certain pests.

- Garlic Extract: Known for its natural antifungal and antibacterial properties, garlic extract can be sprayed on plants to control diseases like downy mildew and bacterial blight.

Mineral-Based Products:

- Copper Sprays: Copper fungicides are effective against a wide range of plant diseases, including bacterial spot and tomato blight. Use formulations approved for organic gardening and apply as directed to avoid potential toxicity to plants and soil microbes.

- Sulfur: Long used in organic farming, sulfur is particularly effective against powdery mildew. It should be used with caution, as high concentrations can be harmful to beneficial insects and plants under certain conditions.

Cultural Practices:

- Crop Rotation: Reduces the buildup of soil-borne pathogens and interrupts disease cycles.

- Proper Spacing: Ensures adequate air circulation, reducing humidity around plants and minimizing the risk of fungal infections.

- Sanitation: Removing and properly disposing of infected plant material prevents the spread of pathogens.

Compost Teas:

- Actively Aerated Compost Tea (AACT): Brewing compost with oxygenated water enhances beneficial microbial activity. When applied to plants, it can improve plant health and resilience against diseases.

Preventive Measures:

- Healthy Soil: Maintaining a vibrant soil ecosystem through organic amendments and mulches supports strong plant growth and natural disease resistance.

- Resistant Varieties: Selecting plant varieties bred for disease resistance is a cornerstone of organic disease prevention.

Monitoring and Early Intervention:

- Regular observation of plants for early signs of disease enables timely application of treatments before significant damage occurs.

By integrating these organic treatment options into a garden management plan, gardeners can effectively control plant diseases in a manner that supports the health of the garden and its environment. Organic disease management is a dynamic process requiring adaptability and a commitment to learning and observation. Through these efforts, sustainable gardening practices not only protect plants but also contribute to the broader health of our planet.

Prevention and Monitoring in Disease Management

Effective disease management in the garden hinges not only on treatment but also on diligent prevention and monitoring. These proactive measures form a critical first line of defense against plant diseases, minimizing the need for intervention and ensuring the health and productivity of the garden. Here's a focused look at the strategies for preventing plant diseases and the importance of regular monitoring.

Preventive Strategies:

- Soil Health: Begin with the foundation of all plant health— the soil. Enriching garden soil with organic matter improves drainage and aeration, reduces compaction, and encourages a vibrant community of beneficial microbes. Healthy soil supports robust plant growth, inherently lessening disease susceptibility.

- Proper Plant Selection: Choose disease-resistant varieties whenever possible. These plants have been bred to resist specific pathogens and offer an invaluable asset in disease prevention. Additionally, selecting plants appropriate for your climate and soil conditions reduces stress on the plants, which can diminish disease occurrence.

- Optimal Planting Practices: Overcrowding can create a microenvironment that favors the development and spread of many diseases. Space plants, according to their mature size, ensure adequate air circulation. Properly spacing plants also allows for more efficient penetration of sunlight, which helps to keep foliage dry and less hospitable to fungal pathogens.

- Water Management: Water plants in the morning to allow foliage to dry before evening. Utilize drip irrigation or soaker hoses to deliver water directly to the soil, minimizing moisture on leaves and thus reducing the risk of fungal diseases. Ensure the garden has adequate drainage to prevent soggy conditions conducive to root rot and other diseases.

- Mulching: Applying organic mulch around plants helps to regulate soil moisture, suppress weeds, and reduce soil splash, which can spread soil-borne pathogens to plant foliage.

Monitoring Techniques:

- Regular Inspection: Conduct thorough inspections of your garden at least once a week. Look for early signs of disease, such as unusual leaf spots, blights, or wilting. Early detection is critical to managing diseases before they become widespread.

- Record-Keeping: Keep detailed records of plant varieties, planting dates, occurrences of disease, and treatment outcomes. This information is invaluable for planning future garden layouts and strategies, as it helps identify patterns and potential disease-resistant varieties.

- Environmental Monitoring: Pay attention to weather conditions, particularly extended periods of humidity or rain, which can precipitate outbreaks of certain diseases. Adjusting cultural practices in anticipation of these conditions can mitigate disease risks.

Integrated Approach: Combine preventive and monitoring strategies with organic treatment options as part of an integrated disease management plan. This holistic approach supports not only the health of individual plants but also the broader ecosystem of your garden.

By prioritizing prevention and staying vigilant through regular monitoring, gardeners can significantly reduce the prevalence and impact of plant diseases. This proactive stance fosters a healthier garden, replete with vigorous plants that can better withstand the challenges diseases pose.

CHAPTER 15
Seasonal Gardening Activities

Spring Gardening Checklist

Spring heralds a time of renewal in the garden, offering a fresh opportunity to cultivate a vibrant and productive space. As the earth thaws and days lengthen, gardeners are presented with the task of preparing their plots for the upcoming growing season. A comprehensive spring gardening checklist not only streamlines the transition from dormancy to growth but also ensures that the garden's foundation is robust and ready for the challenges and rewards of the year. Here is a detailed guide to essential spring gardening activities:

Assessment and Planning:

- Garden Evaluation: Walk through your garden to assess winter damage to plants, structures, and garden beds. Note any necessary repairs or replacements.

- Inventory Supplies: Check your garden tools, seeds, and other supplies. Sharpen tools, restock soil amendments, and purchase seeds or seedlings as needed.

- Design and Layout: Plan your garden layout, considering crop rotation and companion planting to enhance plant health and productivity. Incorporate new plants or garden features you wish to try this year.

Soil Preparation:

- Soil Testing: Conduct a soil test to determine pH and nutrient levels. Amend the soil according to test recommendations to optimize plant health.

- Tilling and Aerating: Loosen the soil in garden beds to improve aeration and drainage. Incorporate organic matter like compost or well-rotted manure to enrich the soil.

Planting:

- Early Season Crops: Sow seeds of cool-season crop directly into the soil as soon as it is workable. Consider planting peas, lettuce, spinach, and radishes.

- Seed Starting Indoors: Start warm-season crops indoors under grow lights if you still need to do so. Tomatoes, peppers, and eggplants require a head start before transplanting outdoors after the last frost.

- Bare-Root Plants: Plant bare-root trees, shrubs, and perennials early in the season before they break dormancy.

Pest and Disease Management:

- Clean-Up: Remove any remaining plant debris from the previous season to reduce disease and pest harborage.

- **Preventative Measures**: Apply organic mulch to suppress weeds and diseases. Consider using natural pest deterrents or barriers as needed.

Irrigation Check:

- **Irrigation System**: Inspect and repair any irrigation systems, hoses, or rain barrels. Ensure everything is in working order for the dry months ahead.

Support Structures:

- **Stakes and Trellises**: Repair or replace any damaged stakes, trellises, or support structures. Installing them early can prevent disturbance to growing plants.

Wildlife and Pollinator Support:

- **Bird and Insect Houses**: Clean out birdhouses and inspect bee hotels or insect houses to ensure they are ready for new occupants.

- **Plant for Pollinators**: Plan to include a variety of flowering plants that bloom at different times throughout the season to attract and support pollinators.

Mulching and Fertilizing:

- **Mulch Application**: Apply a layer of organic mulch around perennials, trees, and shrubs to conserve moisture, suppress weeds, and regulate soil temperature.

- **Fertilize Appropriately**: Based on soil test results, apply a balanced, slow-release organic fertilizer to established plants as they begin active growth.

By meticulously following this spring gardening checklist, gardeners can set the stage for a season filled with growth, health, and abundance. Each task, from soil preparation to planting and pest management, builds upon the next, creating a harmonious system that supports vibrant garden life.

Summer Gardening Tasks

As the garden basks in the full strength of the summer sun, the tasks of the gardener shift to maintenance, monitoring, and mid-season adjustments. The vitality of the garden during these warmer months depends heavily on consistent care and the ability to respond to the garden's evolving needs. Here's a focused exploration of summer gardening tasks that are essential for sustaining a healthy and productive garden through the heat of the season.

Watering and Mulching:

- **Deep Watering**: Ensure plants receive deep, infrequent watering to encourage root growth deeper into the soil, where moisture remains longer. Early morning is the best time to water, reducing evaporation and allowing foliage to dry before nightfall.

- **Mulching**: Apply or replenish mulch around plants to conserve soil moisture, suppress weeds, and keep root systems cool. Organic mulches, such as straw or shredded bark, also contribute to soil health as they decompose.

Pest and Disease Vigilance:

- Regular Inspections: Check plants regularly for signs of pests and diseases. Early detection is crucial for effective management without resorting to harsh chemicals.
- Organic Controls: For aphid management, utilize organic pest control methods, such as insecticidal soaps, neem oil, or biological controls like ladybugs. For diseases, remove and destroy affected plant parts, and consider organic fungicides for severe cases.

Pruning and Deadheading:

- Selective Pruning: Remove any dead or diseased foliage to improve plant health and appearance. Prune to enhance air circulation within the plant canopy, which can help prevent fungal diseases.
- Deadheading: Regularly remove spent flowers to encourage continuous blooming in flowering plants. This practice also directs the plant's energy towards growth and further flower production.

Fertilization:

- Mid-Season Feeding: Give plants a mid-season boost with a side dressing of compost or a balanced organic fertilizer to support continued growth and productivity, especially for heavy feeders like tomatoes and peppers.

Support and Training:

- Staking and Support: Check and adjust supports for tall or vining plants as they grow. Proper support prevents damage from winds or heavy fruit loads.
- Training: Secure vining plants to trellises, cages, or stakes to guide their growth. This not only optimizes garden space but also improves air circulation and sun exposure.

Harvesting:

- Regular Harvesting: Harvest vegetables and fruits as they ripen to encourage further production. Regular harvesting prevents overburdening plants and can prolong the harvesting window.

Succession Planting:

- Continuous Crops: Plant additional seeds of fast-growing crops like lettuces, radishes, and spinach to ensure a continuous harvest throughout the season.

Garden Hygiene:

- Weed Management: Keep on top of weeding, especially after rains, to prevent weeds from competing with your plants for water and nutrients.
- Cleanliness: Keep the garden area free of debris and fallen fruit, which can harbor pests or diseases.

Reflection and Adjustment:

- Garden Journal: Maintain a garden journal to record observations, successes, and areas for improvement. This record is invaluable for planning future garden adjustments and improvements.

By undertaking these summer gardening tasks, gardeners can ensure their gardens not only survive but thrive during the heat of summer. These efforts not only preserve the garden's beauty and yield but also enhance its resilience against the challenges unique to the season.

Fall and Winter Garden Preparation

As the vibrant hues of autumn herald, the close of the growing season, gardeners turn their attention to preparing their gardens for the fall and winter months. This critical phase in the gardening calendar involves a series of meticulous steps designed to protect plants, preserve soil health, and lay the groundwork for the following spring. Here's a comprehensive guide to fall and winter garden preparation, ensuring your garden remains resilient and ready for the year ahead.

Garden Clean-Up:

- Remove Spent Plants: Clear out annuals that have completed their life cycle and remove any diseased or pest-infested plant material to prevent pathogens and pests from overwintering.

- Prune Perennials: Cut back dying perennial foliage to tidy up the garden and reduce habitats for pests and disease. Some perennials may be left intact to provide winter interest and habitat for beneficial insects.

Soil Care:

- Soil Testing: Conduct a soil test to guide any necessary amendments. The off-season is an ideal time for adjusting pH levels and replenishing nutrients depleted during the growing season.

- Amend the Soil: Incorporate organic matter such as compost or well-rotted manure to improve soil structure and fertility. This practice enriches the soil, providing a beneficial environment for next year's plants.

Mulching:

- Apply Protective Mulch: After the first hard frost, apply a layer of mulch to perennial beds, around trees, and in vegetable gardens. Mulch insulates the soil, moderating temperature fluctuations and protecting plant roots from freeze-thaw cycles.

Plant Protection:

- Wrap Tender Trees and Shrubs: Use burlap or tree wrap to shield vulnerable trees and shrubs from winter wind and sun scald.

- Protect Cold-Sensitive Plants: Employ frost cloth or straw to protect overwintering vegetables and sensitive perennials from extreme cold.

Watering:

- Deep Watering: Before the ground freezes, give your garden a thorough watering to ensure plants are well-hydrated for winter. This is especially important for evergreens and newly planted trees and shrubs.

Garden Structures and Tools:

- Repair and Clean Garden Structures: Inspect and repair fences, trellises, and raised beds. Clean and store stakes and supports.

- Tool Maintenance: Clean, sharpen, and oil garden tools before storing them for the winter. This prolongs their life and ensures they are ready for spring.

Planning for Spring:

- Order Bulbs and Seeds: Plan for spring blooms by ordering bulbs and seeds for the upcoming planting season. Fall is the perfect time to plant spring-flowering bulbs such as tulips, daffodils, and alliums.

- Reflect and Record: Review your garden journal, noting successes, challenges, and ideas for next year. Update your garden plans and wish lists accordingly.

Wildlife Considerations:

- Provide for Wildlife: Clean and fill bird feeders, and consider leaving seed heads on some perennials to provide food for birds. Install water sources for wildlife to use during dry winter months.

By meticulously preparing your garden for fall and winter, you safeguard your hard work and set the stage for a thriving and vibrant garden in the spring. These tasks, rooted in the cycles of nature, underscore the gardener's role as a steward of the earth, fostering a garden that thrives in harmony with the environment.

CHAPTER 16
Gardening for Sustainability

Eco-friendly Gardening Practices

Embracing eco-friendly gardening practices is not just a step towards cultivating a green thumb; it's a leap toward ensuring the sustainability and health of our planet. These methods focus on minimizing environmental impact and fostering a harmonious balance within the garden ecosystem. Implementing such practices requires a mindful approach to gardening, where every action is taken with consideration for its long-term effects on the environment. Here's a detailed exploration of sustainable gardening techniques that can make a significant difference.

Soil Health as a Foundation:

- Organic Matter Enrichment: Regularly adding organic matter, such as compost or leaf mold, enhances soil fertility naturally, improving its structure and water retention capabilities. Healthy soil is the foundation of a sustainable garden, supporting vigorous plant growth and a dynamic soil microbiome.

- No-till Gardening: Minimizing or eliminating tilling preserves soil structure, prevents erosion, and protects the living soil community. This practice encourages natural aeration and drainage through the activities of earthworms and other beneficial organisms.

Water Conservation Techniques:

- Rainwater Harvesting: Collecting rainwater in barrels or cisterns for garden use reduces reliance on municipal water systems and ensures plants benefit from natural, soft water.

- Drip Irrigation: This efficient watering method delivers water directly to the base of plants, minimizing waste and evaporation. Paired with appropriate watering schedules, it ensures deep watering that promotes healthy root development.

Integrated Pest Management (IPM):

- Biological Controls: Encouraging or introducing beneficial predators, such as ladybugs for aphid control, supports the natural management of pest populations.

- Physical Barriers: Using row covers, nets, or collars around plants can effectively deter pests without the need for chemical interventions.

Plant Choices for Sustainability:

- Native Planting: Favoring native plants reduces the need for supplemental water, fertilizers, and pesticides, as these species are adapted to local soil and climate conditions.

- Diversity in Planting: A diverse garden, with a mix of annuals, perennials, herbs, and vegetables, creates a resilient ecosystem that is less susceptible to outbreaks of pests and diseases.

Natural Fertilizers and Amendments:

- Composting: Turning kitchen scraps and garden waste into compost not only reduces landfill contributions but also provides a rich, natural fertilizer for the garden.

- Green Manures: Planting cover crops such as clover or vetch can fix nitrogen in the soil, suppress weeds, and improve soil health when turned under before flowering.

Sustainable Garden Design:

- Permaculture Principles: Designing gardens based on permaculture principles emphasizes the creation of self-sustaining ecosystems that mimic natural processes, reducing the need for external inputs.

- Pollinator-Friendly Gardens: Including plants that attract and nourish pollinators contributes to the health of the broader ecosystem, supporting biodiversity.

Chemical-Free Garden Management:

- Avoiding Synthetic Chemicals: Opting for organic pest control solutions and natural fertilizers prevents the accumulation of harmful chemicals in the environment, safeguarding water sources and wildlife.

By adopting eco-friendly gardening practices, gardeners not only contribute to the well-being of their immediate environment but also play a role in the global effort to foster sustainability. These methods, grounded in respect for nature's inherent systems, ensure that our gardens are not just places of beauty and productivity but also bastions of ecological responsibility.

Attracting Beneficial Wildlife

In the pursuit of gardening for sustainability, attracting beneficial wildlife to the garden is a crucial strategy. This method creates a living ecosystem in which every organism is essential to preserving the garden's health and equilibrium. By welcoming beneficial wildlife, gardeners can enhance pollination, pest control, and soil health, reducing the need for chemical interventions. Here's how to transform your garden into a haven for helpful fauna:

Creating Habitats for Pollinators:

- Diverse Plant Selection: Include a diverse range of blooming plants that bloom at various times during the growing season so that pollinators such as bees and butterflies have a constant source of food.

- Native Plants: Prioritize native plants in your garden design. They are adapted to your local climate and soil conditions and often attract native pollinators.

- Avoid Pesticides: Chemical pesticides may harm beneficial insects. To save your pollinator pals, choose organic pest management techniques.

Supporting Birds and Bat Populations:

- Birdhouses and Baths: Install birdhouses, feeders, and baths to attract birds. They play a critical role in pest control by eating a wide range of insects.
- Bat Boxes: Encourage bats, which are excellent natural pest controllers, by placing bat boxes in your garden. A single bat can consume thousands of insects in one night.

Fostering Beneficial Insects:

- Insect Hotels: Create or install insect hotels to provide shelter for beneficial insects like ladybugs, lacewings, and solitary bees.
- Leave Some Leaf Litter: Allow a small area of your garden to remain a bit wild with leaf litter and fallen branches. These areas offer shelter for beneficial insects during the colder months.

Encouraging Soil Health and Worm Activity:

- Composting: Maintain a compost pile to enrich the soil and support a healthy ecosystem below ground, attracting earthworms and other soil organisms that improve soil aeration and nutrient cycling.
- No-till Gardening: Practice no-till gardening methods to preserve the natural structure of the soil and protect the habitat of ground-dwelling beneficials.

Water Features:

- Ponds and Water Gardens: Adding a pond or water garden can attract frogs, toads, and other amphibians, which help control pests. Even a minor water feature can provide essential drinking and bathing spots for wildlife.

Garden Structure Variety:

- Layered Planting: Design your garden with a mix of trees, shrubs, and ground covers to create a variety of habitats and niches for different wildlife species.
- Wildflower Meadows: If space allows, dedicate a section of your garden to wildflowers. This meadow-like setting supports a host of pollinators and beneficial insects.

By integrating these strategies into your garden planning, you create a dynamic, interconnected ecosystem. Attracting beneficial wildlife not only contributes to the sustainability of your garden but also to the broader environmental effort of supporting biodiversity. The presence of birdsong, the fluttering of butterflies, and the busy buzz of bees will not only enhance the natural beauty of your garden but also serve as a reminder of your contribution to a healthier planet.

Creating a Pollinator-Friendly Garden

Establishing a pollinator-friendly garden is an enriching endeavor that significantly contributes to environmental sustainability. Pollinators such as bees, butterflies, birds, and bats are crucial for the reproduction of many flowering plants and the production of a large portion of the fruits and vegetables we consume. However, because of habitat loss, pesticide use, and other environmental stresses, their populations are dropping globally. By designing a garden that attracts and supports these essential creatures, gardeners can play a vital role in conserving biodiversity and ensuring the health of ecosystems.

Diverse Plant Selection:

- To create a haven for pollinators, incorporate a wide variety of plants that bloom at different times throughout the year, providing a consistent source of nectar and pollen. Include native species whenever possible, as these are often more attractive to local pollinators and are well-adapted to the local climate and soil conditions.

Plant in Clusters:

- Planting in clusters rather than singly can make it easier for pollinators to locate and access flowers. Groupings of the same species can create a visually impactful garden design while maximizing the ecological benefits.

Include Plants for All Life Stages:

- Many butterflies and other pollinators have specific plant requirements for laying their eggs and for feeding caterpillars. Including host plants for these life stages, such as milkweed for monarch butterflies, ensures a supportive environment for pollinators from egg to adult.

Reduce or Eliminate Pesticide Use:

- Pesticides can be harmful to pollinators, even when not directly applied to flowers. Opt for organic pest control methods and consider tolerating a reasonable level of pest activity as part of a healthy ecosystem.

Provide Water Sources:

- A shallow water feature, birdbath, or even a simple dish of water can offer pollinators a place to drink and bathe, especially during hot and dry periods. Adding stones or floating plants to water features can provide landing spots for insects and small birds.

Offer Shelter:

- Leave some natural areas in your garden for pollinators to nest and overwinter. This could include areas of undisturbed soil, piles of leaves, or dead wood. Consider installing bee hotels or bird and bat houses to provide additional habitat options.

Avoid Hybrid Plants with Double Flowers:

- While attractive, hybrid plants with double flowers often lack nectar and pollen or have flowers that are difficult for pollinators to access. Choose single-flower varieties to ensure that your garden provides real value to visiting pollinators.

Garden Sustainably:

- Incorporate sustainable gardening practices such as composting, rainwater harvesting, and mulching to improve soil health and water conservation. A healthy garden ecosystem supports robust pollinator populations.

Creating a pollinator-friendly garden is a dynamic process that evolves with the seasons and over the years. It's an opportunity to observe and interact with the natural world closely, contributing to the conservation of pollinator populations. As you watch your garden become a buzzing, fluttering hub of activity, you'll know you're making a difference, fostering a slice of biodiversity that supports the broader web of life on Earth.

CONCLUSION

Starting a journey through the garden is like entering a living tapestry made of intricate patterns created by nature. Each chapter of this guide has served as a stepping stone, guiding you through the myriad aspects of gardening, from the foundational understanding of your space to the intricate dance of cultivating a sustainable ecosystem. As we draw the curtain on this comprehensive exploration, it is essential to reflect on the core principles that have underpinned our journey, weaving them into a cohesive narrative that champions the ethos of harmony, sustainability, and coexistence with nature.

The garden is not merely a collection of plants but a symphony of interactions, a microcosm of the natural world where every leaf, every drop of water, and every grain of soil plays a crucial role. By understanding your garden's unique characteristics, you've laid the groundwork for a thriving green space that respects its inherent beauty and challenges. Soil science has offered a deeper appreciation for the very earth under our feet, revealing the importance of nurturing this foundation for the health of all that grows within it.

The art of composting and the principles of fertilization have highlighted the cycles of life and decay, teaching us that what ends can nourish new beginnings. Watering practices, too, have spoken to the essence of care, emphasizing efficiency and mindfulness in nurturing our green charges. From the diversity of salads to the robustness of tomatoes, onions, and garlic, we've explored the joy of cultivating food, not just for sustenance but for the soul, connecting us to the ancient act of tending the earth.

The journey through the chapters has also been a battle against adversaries, with pests and diseases challenging our resolve. Yet, in these challenges, we've learned the value of resilience and the power of organic solutions that safeguard our gardens without compromising the environment. Seasonal gardening activities have attuned us to the rhythms of nature, reminding us that gardening is not a race but a seasonal dance paced by the natural order of growth, bloom, and rest.

In the final chapters, our focus shifted towards a vision of gardening that extends beyond the immediate confines of our green spaces. Gardening for sustainability has emerged not just as a practice but as a philosophy that embraces eco-friendly practices, attracts beneficial wildlife, and creates pollinator-friendly gardens. This approach has underscored the profound connection between individual actions and global environmental health, illustrating how each garden can be a beacon of biodiversity and a sanctuary for the myriad creatures with whom we share this planet.

As we conclude, let this guide serve not as an end but as a beacon, illuminating the path for your continued journey through the world of gardening. Allow the teachings included in these pages to motivate you to create a sanctuary for all life, not only plants, as evidence of the mutually beneficial interaction between people and the environment. In nurturing our gardens, we nurture ourselves, our communities, and the world at large, sowing the seeds for a future where nature and humanity thrive in unison.

In the end, the act of gardening becomes a reflection of life itself—a cycle of learning, growing, and giving back, rooted in love and respect for the natural world. As you turn each page and plant each seed, remember that you are not just growing plants but nurturing a legacy of environmental stewardship, one that will flourish for generations to come.

ABOUT THE AUTHOR

Maxwell Greenfield has over a decade of expertise in exploring the science and practice of sustainable vegetable gardening. With a solid background in agronomy and a deep passion for biodiversity, he started his career as an environmental consultant, deepening his knowledge and skills in rural settings where he tends to a vegetable garden. This not only enhances his well-being but also serves as a testing ground for his theories and methodologies.

Maxwell's view of vegetable gardening extends beyond simply growing food; it's an invitation to reconnect with the natural rhythms of the earth and to rediscover balance and health by nurturing the soil and the plants it supports. He dedicates his time to promoting eco-friendly cultivation techniques and fostering a deep respect for the soil that sustains life. He encourages everyone to view their green space as a vital contribution to global biodiversity.

Maxwell Greenfield

As an editor, every single review is a crucial support for me.
Your voice can make a difference and help me move forward with my work.
If you believe in the value of what I do and want to help me, please take a moment to share your thoughts.
Your honest and sincere review will be a great help to me, and I will read it very carefully.
I thank you from the bottom of my heart for your valuable contribution.

bit.ly/3T3MsE6

BONUS APPENDIX 1
Conducting Soil pH Tests

Understanding the health of your garden soil for various plant species requires testing its pH. Your soil's acidity or alkalinity can be determined using the pH scale, which runs from 0 to 14. Most plants grow best in soil that ranges from pH 6.0 to 7.0, which is slightly acidic to neutral. Yet, certain plants like environments that are more alkaline or acidic.

Materials Needed for Soil pH Testing:

- A soil pH testing kit or a digital pH meter is readily available at gardening stores.

- A clean, dry container for collecting soil samples.

- Distilled water.

Steps for Conducting a Soil pH Test:

- Sample Collection: Collect soil from several areas of your garden, digging about 5-7 inches deep. Remove any stones or debris. Mix the samples in the container to create a composite sample.

- Preparing the Soil Solution: In a clean container, mix a small amount of the soil with distilled water to create a muddy solution. The exact proportions can vary, but a 1:1 ratio of soil to water is commonly used.

Testing the pH:

- Using a Test Kit: Add the provided test chemical to the soil solution, shake well, and wait for the color change. Compare the color with the provided pH range chart.

- Using a Digital pH Meter: Insert the probe of the meter into the soil solution. Wait until the reading stabilizes to note the pH level.

- Interpreting Results: Check the pH value against the ideal range for your plants. A pH below 7 indicates acidity, and above 7 indicates alkalinity.

Adjusting Soil pH:

- Lowering pH (For Alkaline Soil): Add organic materials like pine needles, sulfur, or peat moss.

- Raising pH (For Acidic Soil): Add lime or wood ash to increase alkalinity.

Maintaining Optimal Soil pH:

Regular testing, at least once a year, is recommended to maintain ideal soil conditions.

Remember that pH adjustment is a gradual process and may require repeated applications over time.

Consider the specific needs of your plants since some may require unique pH levels.

BONUS APPENDIX 2
How to adjust the PH of your garden soil

Adjusting the pH of your garden soil is a crucial step in creating a conducive environment for plant growth. Here's a practical guide based on the pH values you've obtained:

For Acidic Soil (pH below 6.0):

Gradually add garden lime (calcium carbonate) to raise the pH.

Dolomitic lime is recommended if your soil also lacks magnesium.

Apply lime according to package instructions, usually in the fall, to allow it to work into the soil over the winter.

For Alkaline Soil (pH above 7.0):

Add organic matter like peat moss, compost, or well-decomposed manure, which can help lower the pH over time.

Sulfur or aluminum sulfate are more immediate solutions for lowering PH. They should be used carefully, following package directions.

Application Tips:

Spread the amendment evenly over the soil and work it into the top 6 to 8 inches.

For large areas, consider renting a tiller for thorough mixing.

Monitoring and Maintenance:

Retest the soil pH a few months after the initial treatment to assess changes.

pH adjustment is often a gradual process that may require multiple applications over a few seasons.

Remember, the amount of amendment needed depends on your soil type and the current PH. It's always better to make gradual adjustments rather than drastic changes.

BONUS APPENDIX 3
Practical tips for the use of fertilizers

Practical Fertilization Tips Based on Soil Type and Plants:

1. Understanding Soil Types:

Sandy Soil: Light and drains quickly. During the growing season, apply water-soluble fertilizers every two weeks since nutrients quickly leak out. Use one to two pounds for every 100 square feet.

Clay Soil: Dense and retains water. Opt for slow-release granular fertilizers, applied once at the beginning of the growing season. Use 2-3 pounds per 100 square feet to avoid over-concentration.

Loamy Soil: Ideal for most plants. Use a balanced granular fertilizer once or twice a season. Around 2 pounds per 100 square feet should suffice.

2. Plant-Specific Recommendations:

Vegetables: Prefer nitrogen-rich fertilizers. Apply in the early morning or late evening to avoid leaf burn. During peak growing season, fertilize every 4-6 weeks.

Fruiting Plants (Tomatoes, Peppers): Require phosphorus for fruit development. Apply a phosphorus-heavy fertilizer every four weeks during the flowering and fruiting stages.

Leafy Greens (Lettuce, Spinach): Favor nitrogen for leaf growth. Apply a nitrogen-rich fertilizer every three weeks during their growing period.

3. Seasonal Timing:

Spring: Start with a balanced fertilizer to wake up plants from dormancy. Early morning application is best.

Summer: Apply water-soluble fertilizers in the evening to avoid rapid evaporation and stress on plants during hot days.

Fall: Reduce fertilizer use as plants prepare for dormancy. Focus on potassium-rich fertilizers to strengthen roots for winter.

4. Application Techniques:

Liquid Fertilizers: Ideal for quick absorption. Dilute as per instructions and apply directly to the soil at the base of the plant.

Granular Fertilizers: Best for long-term nutrient release. Apply evenly around the plant base and water well to help soil absorption.

Foliar Sprays: Useful for immediate nutrient needs. Spray lightly on leaves during cooler parts of the day.

5. Quantity Guidelines:

General Rule: Follow the "less is more" approach. Over-fertilization can damage plants.

Dilution: Always dilute liquid fertilizers as per the package instructions to prevent plant burn.

Reapplication: Generally, reapply every 4-6 weeks, adjusting based on plant response and growth.

6. Monitoring and Adjusting:

Regularly observe plant health. Yellowing leaves might indicate a nitrogen deficiency, while slow growth could suggest a phosphorus shortage.

Adjust fertilization based on plant feedback. If plants show signs of stress after fertilization, reduce the quantity or frequency.

Remember, every garden is unique. These guidelines serve as a starting point, but observation and adaptation to your specific garden conditions are critical to successful fertilization.

BONUS APPENDIX 4
HOW TO MAKE A GOOD MULCH

Incorporating bark chips, such as pine bark mulch, into your garden as a mulching material can offer several benefits. Pine bark chips are particularly effective in conserving soil moisture and suppressing weeds. However, it's important to note that they can slightly acidify the soil over time, making them suitable for acid-loving plants.

For vegetable gardens, different types of mulch can be beneficial. For instance:

Straw Mulch: Ideal for cucumbers, squash, and tomatoes. It's lightweight and easy to spread, making it great for plants that need frequent access to the soil for harvesting.

Grass Clippings: Suitable for leafy vegetables like lettuce and spinach. They decompose quickly, adding nutrients back into the soil, but should be applied in thin layers to prevent matting.

Compost: An excellent all-around choice, especially for root vegetables like carrots and beets. It improves soil structure and fertility as it breaks down.

When using an irrigation system like soaker hoses or drip irrigation, lay the hoses directly on the soil surface near the plant roots before applying the mulch. This ensures that water reaches the soil directly without being blocked or absorbed by the mulch layer. For larger vegetable plants, consider using heavier mulch like wood chips or bark around the base to maintain moisture and suppress weeds effectively while allowing the irrigation system to function efficiently.

BONUS APPENDIX 5
The different kinds of salads

Iceberg Lettuce

Characteristics: Crisp, tightly packed leaves forming a round head. Known for its crunchy texture.
Sowing & Transplanting: Plant seeds indoors 4-6 weeks before the last frost. Transplant outdoors when seedlings are strong, and temperatures are consistently above freezing.
Care: Prefers well-draining soil and consistent moisture. Mulch to retain moisture.
Companion Plants: Radishes, carrots, and onions deter soil pests.

Romaine Lettuce

Characteristics: Tall, upright leaves with a firm rib down the center. It has a crisp texture and a deep flavor.
Sowing & Transplanting: Start seeds indoors 6-8 weeks before the last frost or direct seed outdoors in early spring or late summer.
Care: Needs well-drained soil, regular watering, and partial shade in hot climates.
Companion Plants: Beans, garlic, and chives help repel aphids.

Butterhead Lettuce (Boston or Bibb)

Characteristics: Soft, buttery-textured leaves forming a loose head. Sweet and tender.
Sowing & Transplanting: Sow seeds directly outdoors in spring or late summer. Can also start indoors and transplant.
Care: Requires consistent moisture and well-draining soil. Tolerates light shade.
Companion Plants: Marigolds and nasturtiums deter beetles and aphids.

Leaf Lettuce (Oak Leaf, Red Leaf)

<u>Characteristics</u>: Loose leaves that grow in a rosette. Comes in green and red varieties. Easy to harvest.
<u>Sowing & Transplanting</u>: Direct sow outdoors in early spring and continue into fall. No need to transplant.
<u>Care</u>: Keep soil moist but not waterlogged. Prefers cool conditions.
<u>Companion Plants</u>: Dill and fennel attract beneficial insects.

Arugula

<u>Characteristics</u>: Peppery flavor, often used in salads and as a garnish. Fast-growing.
<u>Sowing & Transplanting</u>: Direct seed outdoors in early spring or fall. Can be grown in containers.
<u>Care</u>: Water evenly to prevent bitterness. Prefers cooler temperatures.
<u>Companion Plants</u>: Bush beans and beets can share space efficiently.

Endive

<u>Characteristics</u>: Curly leaves with a slightly bitter flavor. Great for mixed salads.
<u>Sowing & Transplanting</u>: Sow seeds in late spring for fall harvest. Transplant when temperatures moderate.
<u>Care</u>: Requires regular watering and may benefit from partial shade in hot climates.
<u>Companion Plants</u>: Thyme and rosemary deter pests.

Escarole

<u>Characteristics</u>: Broad, slightly bitter leaves. Less bitter than endive.
<u>Sowing & Transplanting</u>: Plant in early spring or late summer for a fall harvest.
<u>Care</u>: Prefers rich, well-drained soil and consistent moisture.
<u>Companion Plants</u>: Spinach and Swiss chard can provide shade and moisture retention.

Radicchio

Characteristics: Red-purple leaves with a white vein, offering a bitter and spicy taste.
Sowing & Transplanting: Sow directly in late summer for a fall harvest. Transplant seedlings if started indoors.
Care: Needs well-draining soil and regular watering. Prefers cooler temperatures.
Companion Plants: Peas and beans improve soil nitrogen.

Mizuna

Characteristics: Japanese mustard green, feathery leaves, mild peppery flavor. Tolerant of cold weather.
Sowing & Transplanting: Direct seed in early spring or late summer. Continual harvest possible.
Care: Keep soil consistently moist. Can grow in partial shade.
Companion Plants: Nasturtiums and marigolds deter pests and can improve growth.

Kale (as a salad green)

Characteristics: Hardy leaves, rich in nutrients. Can be used young in salads.
Sowing & Transplanting: Sow directly in early spring or late summer for a fall harvest.
Care: Water regularly and mulch to retain moisture. Prefers full sun to partial shade.
Companion Plants: Aromatic herbs like sage and rosemary deter cabbage moths.

For all types, ensure the soil is rich in organic matter and well-draining. Most lettuce varieties prefer cooler temperatures and may require shade cloth in hot climates to prevent bolting. Regular watering, especially during dry spells, will keep leaves tender and flavorful.

BONUS APPENDIX 6
The various types of tomatoes

Tomatoes are incredibly diverse, with varieties to suit every gardener's taste and climate. Here's a concise guide to some of the main types of tomatoes, their characteristics, planting and transplanting timelines, care tips, and companion planting strategies, including transplanting distances.

Cherry Tomatoes

Characteristics: Small, bite-sized fruits perfect for salads. Fast-growing and often prolific.
Sowing: Start seeds indoors 6-8 weeks before the last frost date.
Transplanting: After all danger of frost has passed, spacing plants 24-36 inches apart.
Care: Provide consistent watering and support with cages or stakes. Full sun is essential.
Companion Plants: Basil, onions, and marigolds deter pests.
Transplanting Distance: 24-36 inches apart in rows spaced about 3 feet apart.

Beefsteak Tomatoes

Characteristics: Large, meaty fruits with a rich flavor, ideal for slicing.
Sowing: Indoors, 6-8 weeks before the last expected frost.
Transplanting: Once frost risk is gone, with 36-48 inches between plants.
Care: Regular watering, avoiding foliage wetting. Use stakes or cages for support.
Companion Plants: Basil and marigolds for pest control.
Transplanting Distance: 36-48 inches apart, ensuring ample space for air circulation.

Heirloom Tomatoes

Characteristics: Offers diverse flavors, colors, and shapes. Prized for their delicious taste.

Sowing: Indoors, about 6-8 weeks before the last frost date.

Transplanting: After frost, spacing varies by variety, but generally 24-36 inches apart.

Care: Staking or caging is recommended; maintain soil moisture and mulch.

Companion Plants: Garlic and chives can repel aphids and other pests.

Transplanting Distance: 24-36 inches apart, depending on the variety's size at maturity.

Roma Tomatoes

Characteristics: Plum-shaped, with fewer seeds. Excellent for sauces and canning.

Sowing: Start seeds indoors 6-8 weeks before the last frost.

Transplanting: Transplant outdoors when frost danger has passed, 24-36 inches apart.

Care: Water evenly, support with stakes or cages, and full sun.

Companion Plants: Basil, carrots, and parsley enhance growth and flavor.

Transplanting Distance: 24-36 inches apart in rows 3 feet apart.

General Care Tips for All Tomato Types:

- Watering: Provide 1-2 inches per week, aiming at the base to avoid wetting leaves.

- Support: Use stakes, cages, or trellises to support plants and improve air circulation.

- Mulching: Apply mulch to retain soil moisture and control weeds.

Companion Planting:

Planting tomatoes with basil, marigolds, and carrots can help repel pests and may enhance the flavor of your tomatoes. Avoid planting tomatoes near corn or potatoes, which can share pests and diseases.

Remember, the key to successful tomato gardening is consistent care, from selecting the right variety for your climate to diligent watering, staking, and monitoring for pests and diseases.

BONUS APPENDIX 7
The various types of onions

Onions are a staple in gardens and kitchens worldwide, valued for their flavor and versatility. Here's a guide to the main types of onions, their characteristics, planting, care, companion planting, and transplanting distances.

Yellow Onions

Characteristics: The most common variety, known for its excellent storage qualities and strong flavor, which becomes milder when cooked.

Sowing: Start seeds indoors 6-8 weeks before the last frost date.

Transplanting: Transplant outdoors when the soil is workable and temperatures are consistently above freezing, usually 4-6 weeks before the last expected frost.

Care: Require full sun, regular watering to keep the soil moist, and a nitrogen-based fertilizer early in the growing season.

Companion Plants: Carrots, beets, and lettuce can deter onion flies.

Transplanting Distance: Space plants 4-6 inches apart in rows 12-18 inches apart.

Red Onions

Characteristics: Known for their vibrant red color and slightly sweet flavor, making them a favorite for salads and grilling.

Sowing and Transplanting: Similar to yellow onions.

Care: Same as yellow onions, with added emphasis on mulching to retain soil moisture.

Companion Plants: Chamomile and summer savory improve growth and flavor.

Transplanting Distance: Same as yellow onions.

White Onions

Characteristics: Have a milder and sweeter flavor, often used in Mexican cuisines. They tend to have a softer texture.

Sowing and Transplanting: Follow the same guidelines as for yellow onions.

Care: Requires consistent moisture and may benefit from a light layer of straw mulch to keep the roots cool.

Companion Plants: Planting with strawberries can help deter pests.

Transplanting Distance: Space 4-6 inches apart, with rows 12-18 inches apart.

Green Onions (Scallions)

Characteristics: Harvested young, they have a milder taste and are used both raw and cooked.

Sowing: Can be direct-seeded outdoors as soon as the soil can be worked in spring.

Transplanting: Not typically transplanted as they are harvested young.

Care: Keep the soil consistently moist and weed-free.

Companion Plants: Plant near tomatoes to repel pests.

Spacing: Thin or plant seeds 2-3 inches apart, with rows 6-8 inches apart.

Shallots

Characteristics: Resemble small, elongated onions but with a milder, sweeter flavor. Often used in fine cooking.

Sowing: Rarely grown from seed and usually planted as sets

Transplanting: In early spring, as soon as the soil is workable.

Care: Require well-draining soil and should be kept moist. Shallots are less demanding than onions regarding fertilizer.

Companion Plants: Pair well with strawberries and cucumbers.

Transplanting Distance: Plant sets 6-8 inches apart in rows that are 12 inches apart.

General Care Tips:

<u>Watering</u>: Onions and their relatives require consistent moisture, especially during bulb formation.

<u>Fertilizing</u>: A balanced fertilizer at planting followed by a nitrogen boost pre-bulbing can support healthy growth.

<u>Mulching</u>: Helps retain soil moisture and suppress weeds.

Pest Management:

<u>Rotation</u>: Avoid planting in the same location year after year to prevent disease.

<u>Hygiene</u>: Remove plant debris to minimize disease and pest habitats.

<u>Barrier</u>: Using physical barriers or row covers can protect young plants from pests.

By understanding the specific needs and characteristics of each onion type, gardeners can enjoy a diverse and successful onion harvest tailored to their culinary preferences and gardening conditions.

BONUS APPENDIX 8
The vegetable garden and moon phases

Planting according to the lunar phases is an ancient practice, hinging on the belief that the Moon's gravitational pull affects moisture in the soil, just as it affects the tides, thereby influencing seed germination and plant growth. Here's a general guide to gardening by the lunar phases:

New Moon to First Quarter (Waxing Crescent)

During this phase, the gravitational pull increases, and there is more moisture in the soil. It is considered an excellent time to plant above-ground crops with external seeds, such as lettuce, spinach, celery, and broccoli. The increasing light from the waxing Moon contributes to leaf growth.

First Quarter to Full Moon (Waxing Gibbous)

The Moon's pull continues to be strong, making this phase ideal for planting above-ground crops, especially those that fruit from their flowers like tomatoes, peas, and beans. The belief is that the increased moonlight creates balanced root and leaf growth.

Full Moon to Last Quarter (Waning Gibbous)

As the Moon's light decreases, it's said to be the best time to plant root crops and perennials, including potatoes, carrots, onions, beets, and other vegetables that grow below the ground. It's also a good phase for transplanting, as the waning light directs energy to the roots.

Last Quarter to New Moon (Waning Crescent)

During this phase, the gravitational pull is weaker, and the moonlight decreases, making it a period for rest and maintenance rather than planting. It's considered an ideal time for weeding, pruning, harvesting, and fertilizing the soil.

While scientific evidence supporting lunar planting is mixed, many gardeners find this method enriches their gardening experience and connects them with the natural world's rhythms. Whether you choose to garden by the Moon's phases or not, paying attention to the cycles of nature can only enhance your gardening practice.

BONUS APPENDIX 9
Weekly sowing, transplanting and garden work calendar

Welcome to the "Planting Calendar" appendix.

This section is designed to provide a comprehensive guide to planting, transplanting, and garden maintenance throughout the year.

Planting is the first step in every horticulturist's journey, marking the beginning of a plant's life cycle and setting the stage for a successful harvest. Understanding the optimal time for planting or transplanting is critical to ensuring robust growth, maximizing yields, and enjoying an abundance of fresh produce.

Given the diversity of climates and growing conditions in Italy, we offer customized calendars for southern, central, and northern regions. Whether you reside in the sunny south, temperate central areas, or cooler northern regions, you will find specific directions that will help you effectively plan and organize activities in your vegetable garden.

From crisp lettuce to juicy tomatoes, sturdy carrots to vibrant peppers, this calendar covers a wide range of popular vegetables, indicating the best times to sow or transplant for optimum results. By following these recommendations and adapting them to local conditions, you will be well-equipped to grow a lush and abundant vegetable garden all year round.

Happy sowing and happy gardening!

N.B. - This calendar is for reference and serves as a general guide. Planting and transplanting times may vary depending on the specific weather conditions from year to year and the varieties of plants chosen. It is always advisable to consult a local source or garden center for more accurate information specific to your geographic area.

NORTHERN REGIONS SOWING-PLANTING CALENDAR

For gardeners in the Northern United States, the growing season is shorter and cooler than in the rest of the country. To make the most of the growing season, strategic planning for sowing and transplanting is necessary. Here's a general guide, but remember, local climate variations and microclimates can influence specific timing.

Week 1 29 December 04 January	**Garden Work**: Review garden notes from the previous year. Plan garden layout and select varieties to plant. **Sowing**: Start slow-growing plants indoors, like leeks and onions.
Week 2 05 January 11 January	**Garden Work**: Order seeds and gardening supplies. Clean and sharpen garden tools. **Sowing**: Start perennial herbs and flowers indoors.
Week 3 12 January 18 January	**Garden Work**: Test the germination rate of leftover seeds. Start designing your garden. **Sowing**: Begin sowing peppers and tomatoes indoors.
Week 4 19 January 25 January	**Garden Work**: Continue planning the garden. Consider companion planting. **Sowing**: Continue sowing tomatoes and peppers if not done in week 3.
Week 5 26 January 01 February	**Garden Work**: Begin to prepare seed starting mix and containers for indoor sowing. **Sowing**: Start artichokes and celery indoors.
Week 6 02 February 08 February	**Garden Work**: Check on indoor seedlings. Ensure they have enough light. **Sowing**: Start eggplants and early lettuce indoors.
Week 7 09 February 15 February	**Garden Work**: Prune fruit trees and berry bushes, weather permitting.
Week 8 16 February 22 February	**Garden Work**: Apply dormant oil to fruit trees to control pests. **Sowing**: Start brassicas (broccoli, cabbage, kale) indoors.
Week 9 23 February 01 March	**Garden Work**: Turn compost pile if weather allows. Check for signs of life in perennials. **Sowing**: Continue sowing brassicas and start some herbs indoors.

Week 10 02 March 08 March	**Garden Work**: Prepare cold frames for early spring planting if applicable. **Sowing**: Direct sow peas outdoors if the soil can be worked and is not frozen. Start lettuce and spinach indoors. **Transplanting**: Begin to harden off seedlings that were started early indoors for eventual outdoor transplanting.
Week 11 09 March 15 March	**Garden Work**: Start hardening off seedlings by exposing them to outdoor conditions for a few hours each day. **Sowing**: If not already done, sow tomatoes, peppers, and eggplants indoors. If the soil is workable, direct sow peas and spinach in the garden.
Week 12 16 March 22 March	**Garden Work**: Prepare garden beds as soon as the soil is dry enough to work—remove weeds and mix in compost. **Sowing**: Continue indoor sowing of warm-season crops. Outdoors, sow radishes and lettuces. **Transplanting**: Begin transplanting hardy seedlings outdoors if conditions allow.
Week 13 23 March 29 March	**Garden Work**: Apply mulch to beds to retain moisture and suppress weeds. Install supports for peas. **Sowing**: Carrots and parsnips outdoors. Indoors, start cucumbers and squash. **Transplanting**: Continue transplanting any hardened-off seedlings outdoors.
Week 14 30 March 05 April	**Garden Work**: Check for and manage pests on early-sprouting plants. Continue soil preparation for upcoming plantings. **Sowing**: Direct sow beets and Swiss chard. Indoors, sow annual flowers. **Transplanting**: If weather permits, transplant broccoli, cabbage, and other brassicas outside.

Week 15 06 April 12 April	**Garden Work**: Begin to water garden beds as necessary. **Sowing**: Direct sow leafy greens and continue indoor sowing for succession planting. **Transplanting**: Start transplanting lettuce and spinach if they were started indoors.
Week 16 13 April 19 April	**Garden Work**: Install trellises for peas and other climbers. Begin regular weeding and watering schedule. **Sowing**: Direct sow onions set and potatoes. **Transplanting**: Transplant hardened-off tomatoes, peppers, and eggplants if the weather forecast is stable.
Week 17 20 April 26 April	**Garden Work**: Begin to apply organic fertilizer to early plantings as needed. **Sowing**: Directly sow annual herbs and continue sowing root vegetables. **Transplanting**: Continue with the transplanting of any remaining hardened-off seedlings.
Week 18 27 April 03 May	**Garden Work**: Harden off summer crops like cucumbers, squash, and melons. **Sowing**: Directly sow corn and beans if soil temperature is adequate. **Transplanting**: Start transplanting cucumbers, squash, and other warm-season crops, depending on local frost dates.
Week 19 04 May 10 May	**Garden Work**: Stake tomatoes and start regular inspections for pests and diseases. **Sowing**: Directly sow more beans, cucumbers, and squash for succession crops. **Transplanting**: Ensure all tender plants are now in the ground, post-last frost date.
Week 20 11 May 17 May	**Garden Work**: Add mulch around new transplants to conserve moisture and suppress weeds. **Sowing**: This is the last call for direct sowing of early spring crops. Continue sowing warm-season crops directly in the soil. **Transplanting**: Finish transplanting any indoor-started plants outside.

Week 21 18 May 24 May	**Garden Work**: Apply compost or a balanced organic fertilizer to support the growth of established plants. **Sowing**: Direct sow warm-season crops such as beans, cucumbers, and squash if not already done. Plant successive crops of lettuce and greens to ensure continuous harvest. **Transplanting**: Transplant pumpkin, watermelon, and other melons if not already in the ground.
Week 22 26 May 31 May	**Garden Work**: Mulch around new plantings to conserve moisture and suppress weeds. Start regular pest and disease inspections. **Sowing**: Continue sowing beans, carrots, and sweet corn for succession harvesting. **Transplanting**: Ensure all warm-season transplants like tomatoes, peppers, and eggplants are in the ground.
Week 23 01 June 07 June	**Garden Work**: Increase watering as temperatures rise. Stake or cage tomatoes and provide support for climbing beans and cucumbers. **Sowing**: Direct sow beets and chard for a fall harvest. Plant a second round of corn for succession. **Transplanting**: This is the last chance to transplant any remaining warm-season crops outside.
Week 24 08 June 14 June	**Garden Work**: If necessary, begin thinning fruit on fruit trees. Also, keep an eye on water levels, especially during hot weather. **Sowing**: You can sow herbs like basil outdoors. It's also a good time to sow flowers for late summer and fall blooms.
Week 25 15 June 21 June	**Garden Work**: Start side-dressing crops with organic fertilizer as they begin to flower and set fruit. **Sowing**: Direct sow falls crops like carrots, turnips, and rutabagas. Continue sowing lettuce and greens in shaded areas or use shade cloth to prevent bolting.
Week 26 22 June 28 June	**Garden Work**: Prune any unnecessary growth on tomatoes and check for pests like aphids and spider mites. **Sowing**: Sow more beans for a late summer harvest—plant fast-growing crops like radishes between slower-growing vegetables. **Transplanting**: If you have any late warm-season crops still indoors, it's now or never for transplanting.

Week 27 29 June 05 July	**Garden Work**: Continue monitoring for pests and diseases. Adjust staking and support structures as plants grow. **Sowing**: Direct sow kale, collards, and other hearty greens for a fall harvest.
Week 28 06 July 12 July	**Garden Work**: Begin harvesting early crops like peas and lettuces. Maintain watering, especially during dry spells. **Sowing**: Sow beets and turnips for a fall crop. Also, a good time for another round of herbs.
Week 29 13 July 19 July	**Garden Work**: Deadhead flowers to encourage new blooms. Start collecting seeds from early-season crops. **Sowing**: For continuous harvests, sow fast-growing, heat-tolerant greens like Swiss chard and leaf lettuce.
Week 30 20 July 26 July	**Garden Work**: Apply a layer of compost to beds that have finished producing to prepare for late-season crops. **Sowing**: Last chance to sow crops for a fall harvest, including carrots, beets, and leafy greens.
Week 31 27 July 02 August	**Garden Work**: Begin planning your fall garden. Continue monitoring for pests and diseases. Keep up with weeding and watering, especially during dry spells. **Sowing**: Sow fall crops such as spinach, kale, and other leafy greens—direct sow radishes and turnips. **Transplanting**: Plant out broccoli, cauliflower, and cabbage seedlings for a fall harvest.
Week 32 03 August 09 August	**Garden Work**: Start saving seeds from your favorite plants. Continue deadheading flowers and harvesting vegetables as they mature. **Sowing**: Direct sow beets and carrots for a fall harvest. Continue planting lettuce and other greens in shaded areas. **Transplanting**: Last chance for transplanting brussels sprouts and winter cabbages.
Week 33 10 August 16 August	**Garden Work**: Prune summer-fruiting raspberries after harvest. Keep watering regularly but be mindful of water conservation. **Sowing**: Sow arugula, mustard greens, and other quick-growing cool-season crops. **Transplanting**: This is not typically a time for transplanting as the focus shifts towards fall crops.

Week 34 17 August 23 August	**Garden Work**: Begin to clear out spent summer crops and prepare beds for fall planting. Add compost or other organic matter to refresh the soil. **Sowing**: Continue sowing leafy greens and root vegetables for fall harvesting. Plant garlic for next year's harvest.
Week 35 24 August 30 August	**Garden Work**: Mulch newly planted fall crops to retain moisture and control soil temperature. Start collecting herbs for drying. **Sowing**: Final chance to sow quick-growing crops that can mature before the first frost.
Week 36 31 August 06 September	**Garden Work**: Begin fall cleanup in the garden. Remove any diseased plants and compost healthy ones. **Sowing**: Sow cover crops in empty beds to improve soil health over winter.
Week 37 07 September 13 September	**Garden Work**: Continue harvesting mature vegetables. Start planning for winter protection of perennial plants. **Sowing**: Too late for sowing most crops, focus on preparing for next season.
Week 38 14 September 20 September	**Garden Work**: Plant spring-flowering bulbs. Keep watering and weeding as necessary. **Sowing**: Not advisable for vegetables; focus might shift to ornamental garden planning.
Week 39 21 September 27 September	**Garden Work**: Prepare for the first frost by having covers ready for sensitive crops. Begin to reduce watering to harden off plants. **Sowing**: Not recommended as the growing season winds down.
Week 40 28 September 04 October	**Garden Work**: After the first frost, clean up the garden. Remove all annuals and harvest mature vegetables.
Week 41 05 October 11 October	**Garden Work**: Continue cleaning up the garden, removing spent annuals and vegetables. Start adding compost and mulch to prepare beds for winter.
Week 42 12 October 18 October	**Garden Work**: Plant garlic cloves for next year's harvest. Winterize irrigation systems and water features. **Sowing**: Consider sowing cover crops in empty beds to improve soil over winter if not already.

Week 43	**Garden Work**: Rake up fallen leaves and add them to compost piles. Protect sensitive perennials with mulch or burlap wraps.
19 October 25 October	
Week 44 26 October 01 November	**Garden Work**: Finalize any mulching and protection of garden beds. Ensure all tender plants are brought indoors or are adequately covered.
Week 45 02 November 08 November	**Garden Work**: Clean and store garden tools. Begin planning next year's garden, noting what worked and what didn't.
Week 46 09 November 15 November	**Garden Work**: Continue tool maintenance. Check stored bulbs and tubers for rot and discard any that are not viable.
Week 47 16 November 22 November	**Garden Work**: Start indoor gardening projects like growing herbs on windowsills. Review garden catalogs for next season's planning.
Week 48 23 November 29 November	**Garden Work**: Secure winter protections for gardens, such as burlap screens for wind protection.
Week 49 30 November 06 December	**Garden Work**: Check on overwintering plants and apply water if pots are dry. Ensure protective coverings are secure.
Week 50 07 December 13 December	**Garden Work**: Monitor for rodent activity near stored bulbs or in the garden. Adjust winter protections as needed.
Week 51 14 December 20 December	**Garden Work**: Ideal time for planning the next year's garden. Consider rotating crops and trying new varieties.
Week 52 21 December 27 December	**Garden Work**: Reflect on the past gardening year and update gardening journals with notes and plans for the upcoming season.

MIDDLE REGIONS SOWING-PLANTING CALENDAR

Creating a gardening calendar for the Central United States involves adapting to a climate that can experience extreme variations, from hot summers to cold winters. This guide is a basic outline; specific planting times can vary based on your exact location within the Central region and the current year's weather conditions.

Week 1 29 December 04 January	**Garden Work**: Review seed catalogs and plan the garden layout. Order seeds. **Sowing**: Start seeds indoors for cold-tolerant vegetables like kale and broccoli.
Week 2 05 January 11 January	**Garden Work**: Check on any overwintering plants in the greenhouse or indoors. **Sowing**: Continue starting seeds indoors for cool-season crops.
Week 3 12 January 18 January	**Garden Work**: Organize garden tools and supplies. Clean and sharpen tools. **Sowing**: Sow herbs and lettuce indoors under grow lights.
Week 4 19 January 25 January	**Garden Work**: Test soil samples from your garden and adjust amendments accordingly. **Sowing**: Start onion seeds indoors.
Week 5 26 January 01 February	**Garden Work**: Plan irrigation or watering systems for the upcoming season. **Sowing**: Begin sowing tomato and pepper seeds indoors. **Transplanting**: Transplant any indoor-grown seedlings to larger pots if necessary.
Week 6 02 February 08 February	**Garden Work**: Apply mulch to perennials or cold-hardy crops outdoors if weather permits. **Sowing**: Start more lettuce and spinach indoors. **Transplanting**: Carefully transplant any robust seedlings to individual pots.
Week 7 09 February 15 February	**Garden Work**: Prune dormant fruit trees and berry bushes, weather permitting. **Sowing**: Continue indoor sowing of cool-season vegetables.

Week 8 16 February 22 February	**Garden Work**: Prepare raised beds and garden plots if the ground is workable. **Sowing**: Sow peas indoors or outdoors if the soil is not frozen.
Week 9 23 February 01 March	**Garden Work**: Begin hardening off seedlings by exposing them to outdoor conditions for short periods. **Sowing**: Direct sow radishes and carrots in prepared beds, weather permitting.
Week 10 02 March 08 March	**Garden Work**: Clean out birdhouses and set up new ones. Continue preparing garden beds. **Sowing**: Direct sow parsnips and turnips if soil and weather allow. Continue indoor sowing as needed. **Transplanting**: Transplant any ready, hardened-off cool-season seedlings outdoors.
Week 11 09 March 15 March	**Garden Work**: Continue to prepare garden beds, adding compost or other amendments. **Sowing**: If the soil is workable, sow peas, spinach, and lettuce directly into the garden. If not already done, start tomato, pepper, and eggplant seeds indoors. **Transplanting**: Begin transplanting early seedlings like cabbage and broccoli into the garden, depending on weather conditions.
Week 12 16 March 22 March	**Garden Work**: Weed and mulch around perennials as needed. Install trellises or supports for peas and climbing vegetables. **Sowing**: Direct sow radishes, carrots, and beets in the garden. If your growing season is longer indoors, continue starting seeds of warm-season crops. **Transplanting**: Transplant lettuce and other leafy greens outdoors under protection if frost is still a threat.
Week 13 23 March 29 March	**Garden Work**: Prune spring-flowering shrubs after they bloom. Continue bed preparation for summer crops. **Sowing**: Directly sow more root crops and cool-season greens. In warmer parts, start sowing warm-season crops like beans and corn directly into the garden. **Transplanting**: If the weather is warm enough, begin hardening off and transplanting tomatoes, peppers, and eggplants.

Week 14 30 March 05 April	**Garden Work**: Apply balanced fertilizer to fruit trees and berry bushes. Set up rain barrels to conserve water. **Sowing**: Continue direct sowing of cool and warm-season vegetables as appropriate for your area. Sow sunflowers and other annual flowers. **Transplanting**: Continue transplanting hardened-off vegetables and herbs.
Week 15 06 April 12 April	**Garden Work**: Start regular weeding sessions to keep beds clear. As pests begin to appear, consider applying organic pest control measures. **Sowing**: Direct sow squash, cucumbers, and melons if soil temperatures are warm enough. Plant potatoes. **Transplanting**: Transplant any remaining seedlings that have been hardened off.
Week 16 13 April 19 April	**Garden Work**: Install stakes or cages for tomatoes and other plants that will need support. **Sowing**: Direct sow more beans, corn, and any remaining warm-season crops. **Transplanting**: Continue transplanting any seedlings that are ready and have been adequately hardened off.
Week 17 20 April 26 April	**Garden Work**: Begin monitoring for pest and disease issues. Use floating row covers to protect young plants from pests. **Sowing**: Direct sow herbs like basil and cilantro. Continue sowing successions of lettuce and greens. **Transplanting**: Finish transplanting any remaining tomatoes, peppers, and eggplants.
Week 18 27 April 03 May	**Garden Work**: Thin seedlings from direct-sown crops like carrots and beets to give them room to grow. **Sowing**: Start succession sowing of crops like beans and corn for continuous harvests. **Transplanting**: Begin transplanting cucumbers, squash, and melons if you haven't already.

Week 19 04 May 10 May	**Garden Work**: Add mulch to conserve moisture and suppress weeds. Set up soaker hoses or drip irrigation for efficient watering. **Sowing**: Direct sow pumpkins and gourds for fall harvest. **Transplanting**: Ensure all summer crops are in the ground.
Week 20 11 May 17 May	**Garden Work**: Check irrigation systems and make adjustments for the growing season. Begin regular fertilization of vegetables. **Sowing**: Continue succession planting of quick-growing crops like radishes and lettuces. **Transplanting**: No specific transplanting tasks unless replacing failed plants or adding new additions.
Week 21 18 May 24 May	**Garden Work**: Check plants regularly for pests and diseases. Apply organic pest control methods as needed. Continue mulching to conserve moisture. **Sowing**: Direct sow or sow in succession beans, corn, and cucumbers for continuous harvests. **Transplanting**: If not done already, finish transplanting any warm-season crops like tomatoes, peppers, cucumbers, and melons.
Week 22 25 May 31 May	**Garden Work**: Increase watering as temperatures rise. To encourage growth, start side-dressing vegetables with compost or a balanced fertilizer. **Sowing**: Plant heat-tolerant greens like Swiss chard and New Zealand spinach. Continue succession planting of beans and corn. **Transplanting**: Transplant any remaining seedlings that have been hardened off.
Week 23 01 June 07 June	**Garden Work**: Install shade cloths over sensitive crops to protect them from intense midday sun. Begin harvesting early crops like lettuce and radishes. **Sowing**: Direct sow okra and sweet potatoes if not already done. **Transplanting**: No specific transplanting tasks unless filling in gaps or replacing failed plants.

Week 24 08 June 14 June	**Garden Work**: Watch watering, especially for container plants. Pinch back herbs like basil to encourage bushier growth.
	Sowing: Sow fast-growing crops like radishes and turnips between slower-growing vegetables.
Week 25 15 June 21 June	**Garden Work**: Start staking and supporting plants that are getting larger. Weed regularly to prevent competition for nutrients and water.
	Sowing: Continue succession sowing of crops for continuous harvests. Consider a last planting of corn for late summer harvest.
Week 26 22 June 28 June	**Garden Work**: Begin regular pest and disease inspections as soon as the garden is in full swing. Water deeply and less frequently to encourage root growth.
	Sowing: Last chance for sowing beans for a final harvest before fall.
Week 27 29 June 05 July	**Garden Work**: Harvest early morning to keep plants healthy and productive. Begin canning, freezing, or drying surplus produce.
	Sowing: Direct sow carrots and beets for a fall harvest.
	Transplanting: May transplant perennial herbs or flowers, but focus is on vegetable maintenance.
Week 28 06 July 12 July	**Garden Work**: Apply mulch to keep soil temperature stable and conserve water. Continue harvesting crops as they mature.
	Sowing: Plant fall crops like kale, collards, and turnips.
	Transplanting: Start planning fall garden layouts and prepare areas for late-season transplants.
Week 29 13 July 19 July	**Garden Work**: Monitor water needs closely, especially during hot, dry periods. Start saving seeds from early crops.
	Sowing: Sow spinach, lettuce, and other cool-season crops in shaded areas or with sun protection for a fall harvest.
	Transplanting: It is too hot for most transplants; focus on watering and pest control.
Week 30 20 July 26 July	**Garden Work**: Begin to plan for fall gardening activities. Keep harvesting, especially tomatoes, to encourage new fruit to set.
	Sowing: Last call for sowing certain root crops and greens for a fall harvest.

Week 31 27 July 02 August	**Garden Work**: Continue deep watering during dry spells. Begin planning for fall vegetable gardening. Keep weeding to minimize competition for nutrients. **Sowing**: Direct sow falls crops like beets, carrots, and turnips. **Transplanting**: Start transplanting seedlings for your fall garden, such as broccoli and cabbage.
Week 32 03 August 09 August	**Garden Work**: Harvest early-maturing vegetables. Prune tomato plants by removing lower leaves to prevent disease and improve air circulation. **Sowing**: For a fall harvest, sow leafy greens like spinach and kale in a shaded area or with sun protection. **Transplanting**: Continue with fall vegetable transplants, ensuring they're watered well to establish.
Week 33 10 August 16 August	**Garden Work**: Start saving seeds from summer crops. Keep watering deeply, especially for new transplants. **Sowing**: Sow radishes and lettuce for a quick crop before cold weather. **Transplanting**: Transplant any remaining fall crops, focusing on leafy greens and brassicas.
Week 34 17 August 23 August	**Garden Work**: Begin preparing soil for next season by adding compost or manure. Start dividing perennials. **Sowing**: Final chance to sow crops for fall harvesting, including fast-maturing greens and radishes. **Transplanting**: This is the last chance for transplanting fall crops if the weather allows.
Week 35 24 August 30 August	**Garden Work**: Keep monitoring for pests and diseases. Remove any spent plants and compost healthy remains. **Sowing**: Sow cover crops in areas of the garden that will be left fallow over winter.
Week 36 31 August 06 September	**Garden Work**: Start collecting and drying herbs for winter use. Begin fall clean-up in the garden. **Sowing**: In warmer parts of the central region, you can still sow quick-maturing greens.

Week 37 07 September 13 September	**Garden Work**: Test soil and adjust pH or nutrient levels as needed. Continue harvesting mature vegetables. **Sowing**: Plant garlic cloves for next year's harvest.
Week 38 14 September 20 September	**Garden Work**: Apply mulch to protect soil and suppress weeds. Harvest winter squash and pumpkins. **Sowing**: Last chance to sow cover crops before it gets too cold.
Week 39 21 September 27 September	**Garden Work**: Continue garden cleanup. Protect sensitive plants from early frosts with covers.
Week 40 28 September 04 October	**Garden Work**: Plant spring-flowering bulbs. Water trees and shrubs deeply before the ground freezes.
Week 41 05 October 11 October	**Garden Work**: Continue to water perennials and newly planted trees or shrubs. Add mulch to protect plants from the upcoming cold.
Week 42 12 October 18 October	**Garden Work**: Rake and remove fallen leaves, or use them as mulch. Begin to winterize garden tools and irrigation systems. **Sowing**: Consider planting garlic for next year's harvest if not done last week.
Week 43 19 October 25 October	**Garden Work**: Apply a final layer of mulch to perennial beds for winter protection. Drain and store hoses.
Week 44 26 October 01 November	**Garden Work**: Clean out annual beds, removing spent plants to reduce pest issues next year.
Week 45 02 November 08 November	**Garden Work**: Protect sensitive plants from frost. Ensure all garden equipment is cleaned and stored properly. **Sowing**: No outdoor sowing. Consider starting some herbs or greens indoors if you have grown lights.
Week 46 09 November 15 November	**Garden Work**: Check stored bulbs and tubers for rot or drying out. Continue protecting plants from freezing temperatures.

Week 47 16 November 22 November	**Garden Work**: Finalize any garden cleanup before snowfall. Secure protective coverings for plants that remain outside.
Week 48 23 November 29 November	**Garden Work**: Check on winterized garden tools and equipment. Plan next year's garden layout and plant selections.
Week 49 30 November 06 December	**Garden Work**: Ensure mulch is in place to protect plant roots from freezing. Consider feeding birds to encourage them to visit your garden next year.
Week 50 07 December 13 December	**Garden Work**: Browse seed catalogs and websites to plan for spring. Check on any overwintering plants in storage.
Week 51 14 December 20 December	**Garden Work**: Great time for reading gardening books and expanding your knowledge. Check indoor plants for pests.
Week 52 21 December 27 December	**Garden Work**: Reflect on the past gardening year and make notes for improvements or changes for next year.

SOUTHERN REGIONS SOWING-PLANTING CALENDAR

Creating a comprehensive gardening calendar for the Southern United States involves understanding the region's unique climate, which allows for a wide range of vegetables to be sown and transplanted throughout the year. Here is a simplified version, highlighting key vegetables for each month. This guide is meant to offer a general overview; specific planting times can vary based on your exact location and current weather conditions.

Week 1 29 December 04 January	**Garden Work**: Clean and sharpen garden tools. **Sowing**: Indoors, start seeds for cool-season vegetables like lettuce, kale, and spinach.
Week 2 05 January 11 January	**Garden Work**: Test soil pH and adjust as necessary. Continue planning your garden. **Sowing**: Start broccoli, cabbage, and cauliflower seeds indoors.
Week 3 12 January 18 January	**Garden Work**: Clean up garden beds, removing any debris or dead plants. **Sowing**: Sow cool-season vegetable seeds indoors. Consider starting some herbs indoors.
Week 4 19 January 25 January	**Garden Work**: Apply mulch to perennial beds to protect against late frost. **Sowing**: Indoors, continue sowing cool-season crops. Start tomato and pepper seeds indoors. **Transplanting**: If weather permits, you can transplant overwintered perennials.
Week 5 26 January 01 February	**Garden Work**: Prune dormant trees and shrubs, except for spring bloomers. **Sowing**: Continue starting seeds indoors for spring planting. **Transplanting**: Start hardening off cool-season seedlings for transplanting in a few weeks.
Week 6 02 February 08 February	**Garden Work**: Prepare raised beds and garden plots by adding compost and organic matter. **Sowing**: Direct sow peas, radishes, and turnips outdoors if the soil is workable. **Transplanting**: Begin transplanting cool-season crops outdoors under protection if needed.

Week 7 09 February 15 February	**Garden Work**: Weed and prepare more beds. Apply fertilizer to fruit trees. **Sowing**: Direct sow carrots, beets, and lettuce outdoors. Start squash and cucumbers indoors. **Transplanting**: Transplant hardened-off seedlings of cool-season vegetables outdoors.
Week 8 16 February 22 February	**Garden Work**: Set up trellises for peas and vining plants. Begin spring cleanup. **Sowing**: Continue direct sowing of cool-season vegetables as the weather allows. **Transplanting**: Transplant strawberry plants and bare-root trees as soil and weather permits.
Week 9 23 February 01 March	**Garden Work**: Apply pre-emergent herbicides to beds if needed. Start regular watering schedules as the weather warms. **Sowing**: Direct sow more rounds of cool-season crop for succession planting. Indoors, start eggplants and more tomatoes if needed. **Transplanting**: Continue transplanting any ready seedlings outdoors with frost protection methods in place.
Week 10 02 March 08 March	**Garden Work**: Begin mulching to conserve moisture and suppress weeds. **Sowing**: In warmer parts, start sowing warm-season crops like beans and corn directly into the ground. **Transplanting**: Transplant any remaining cool-season crops and early-started warm-season crops like tomatoes and peppers, using row covers if frost is still a threat.
Week 11 09 March 15 March	**Garden Work**: Continue weeding and preparing beds. Test soil if not already done. **Sowing**: Direct sow warm-season vegetables like squash, cucumbers, and beans. Plant more rounds of leafy greens. **Transplanting**: Begin transplanting tomato, pepper, and eggplant seedlings outdoors if the frost danger has passed.

Week 12 16 March 22 March	**Garden Work**: Install support structures for peas, beans, and tomatoes. **Sowing**: Direct sow corn, okra, and sunflowers. Plant herb seeds like basil and cilantro. **Transplanting**: Continue transplanting any started warm-season crops.
Week 13 23 March 29 March	**Garden Work**: Mulch around new transplants to conserve moisture. **Sowing**: Start a new round of leafy greens in shaded areas to extend harvests into warmer months. **Transplanting**: Transplant melons and cucumbers if not done previously.
Week 14 30 March 05 April	**Garden Work**: Begin regular pest and disease inspections. **Sowing**: Direct sow or plant seedlings for heat-tolerant greens like Swiss chard. **Transplanting**: Ensure all frost-sensitive plants are in the ground, as frost dates should now be past.
Week 15 06 April 12 April	**Garden Work**: Start a fertilizing schedule for fast-growing vegetable crops. **Sowing**: Sow another round of corn and beans for succession harvesting. **Transplanting**: It's a good time to transplant herbs into the garden.
Week 16 13 April 19 April	**Garden Work**: Increase watering as temperatures start to rise. **Sowing**: Direct sow more root crops such as carrots and beets for continuous harvests. **Transplanting**: If needed, transplant any late-started seedlings outdoors.
Week 17 20 April 26 April	**Garden Work**: Begin thinning seedlings to the proper spacing. **Sowing**: Direct sow summer squash and more beans. **Transplanting**: Keep transplanting any remaining seedlings, focusing on summer crops.
Week 18 27 April 03 May	**Garden Work**: Apply mulch to new plantings to prevent weeds. **Sowing**: Start seeds for fall crops indoors like broccoli and cauliflower. **Transplanting**: Transplant any late peppers, tomatoes, and eggplants.

Week 19 04 May 10 May	**Garden Work**: Continue pest control and disease management. **Sowing**: In warmer areas, start sowing heat-loving herbs like basil directly outdoors. **Transplanting**: Begin moving fall crops from seed trays to larger pots if started indoors.
Week 20 11 May 17 May	**Garden Work**: Harvest early spring crops like lettuce and radishes. **Sowing**: Direct sow more carrots, turnips, and radishes for a continuous supply. **Transplanting**: Ensure all remaining warm-season crops are planted out.
Week 21 18 May 24 May	**Garden Work**: Start regular weeding to keep plants healthy and unobstructed. **Sowing**: Direct sow sweet potatoes if they haven't already been done. This is also a good time to plant sunflowers in the final stage. **Transplanting**: Plant out any remaining summer seedlings, such as cucumbers, if not already in the ground.
Week 22 25 May 31 May	**Garden Work**: Increase watering frequency as the weather warms, especially for newly transplanted seedlings. **Sowing**: Direct sow okra and southern peas for a summer harvest. Continue sowing herbs like basil in pots. **Transplanting**: No major transplanting tasks this week unless replacing spent spring crops with summer varieties.
Week 23 01 June 07 June	**Garden Work**: Apply mulch to conserve moisture during hot weather. **Sowing**: Sow pumpkins and winter squash for a fall harvest. **Transplanting**: Consider transplanting heat-tolerant greens in shaded spots.
Week 24 08 June 14 June	**Garden Work**: Monitor for pests and diseases; use organic control methods as needed. **Sowing**: Direct sow beans and corn for a late summer harvest. **Transplanting**: Replace any underperforming plants with heat-tolerant varieties.

Week 25 15 June 21 June	**Garden Work**: Harvest early summer crops like tomatoes and peppers. **Sowing**: Start seeds for fall vegetables indoors, such as broccoli, cabbage, and kale. **Transplanting**: No major transplanting tasks unless filling gaps in the garden.
Week 26 22 June 28 June	**Garden Work**: Continue harvesting and managing pests and diseases. **Sowing**: Plant more heat-tolerant herbs like basil or cilantro in the shade. **Transplanting**: Still time to plant more heat-tolerant vegetable transplants if needed.
Week 27 29 June 05 July	**Garden Work**: Start planning for fall gardening; prepare beds as early crops are harvested. **Sowing**: In very hot areas, consider sowing heat-tolerant greens or a quick crop of beans. **Transplanting**: Begin transplanting early-started fall crops into cooler, prepared beds.
Week 28 06 July 12 July	**Garden Work**: Keep the garden well-watered, especially during periods of low rain. **Sowing**: Sow fall crops like squash and cucumbers in cooler areas. **Transplanting**: Transplant fall crops such as broccoli and cabbage if started indoors.
Week 29 13 July 19 July	**Garden Work**: Continue weeding and mulching to keep soil moist and cool. **Sowing**: Direct sow beets and carrots for fall harvesting. **Transplanting**: Move fall seedlings outdoors, ensuring they have shade and water.
Week 30 20 July 26 July	**Garden Work**: Begin to clear out spent summer crops and prepare beds for more fall planting. **Sowing**: Directly sow leafy greens like spinach and kale in shaded areas or with sun protection. **Transplanting**: Continue transplanting any remaining fall crops.

Week 31 27 July 02 August	**Garden Work**: Maintain consistent watering, especially for new transplants. Start seed saving from early crops. **Sowing**: Direct sow squash, cucumbers, and beans for a late harvest. **Transplanting**: Begin to transplant fall crops like broccoli, cabbage, and kale.
Week 32 03 August 09 August	**Garden Work**: Add mulch to keep soil moist and cool, important for germinating seeds and young plants. **Sowing**: Continue sowing carrots, beets, and turnips directly in the garden. **Transplanting**: Plant more heat-tolerant greens in areas shaded from the intense afternoon sun.
Week 33 10 August 16 August	**Garden Work**: Prune tomato plants to remove diseased foliage and improve air circulation. **Sowing**: Start seeds for brussels sprouts and winter squash indoors. **Transplanting**: Transplant leeks and late cabbage for a fall harvest.
Week 34 17 August 23 August	**Garden Work**: Begin prepping beds for late fall and winter crops, adding compost and organic matter. **Sowing**: Sow spinach, kale, and other leafy greens for a fall harvest. **Transplanting**: Continue transplanting fall and winter crops outdoors.
Week 35 24 August 30 August	**Garden Work**: Monitor for pests and diseases; apply organic treatments as necessary. **Sowing**: Direct sow radishes and lettuce for a quick fall crop. **Transplanting**: No major transplanting tasks; focus on ensuring newly planted seedlings are well-watered.
Week 36 31 August 06 September	**Garden Work**: Start clearing summer crops that are finishing up to make room for fall and winter vegetables. **Sowing**: In cooler parts of the region, begin sowing garlic for next year's harvest. **Transplanting**: Plant strawberry plants for a spring harvest.

Week 37 07 September 13 September	**Garden Work**: Keep the garden tidy by removing fallen leaves and debris to prevent disease. **Sowing**: Direct sow cool-weather crops like turnips, mustard greens, and Swiss chard. **Transplanting**: Move cool-season crop seedlings outdoors, ensuring they have shade from the still-strong sun.
Week 38 14 September 20 September	**Garden Work**: Begin to water less frequently as the weather cools, but ensure soil remains moist for germinating seeds. **Sowing**: Plant cover crops in empty beds to improve soil over winter. **Transplanting**: Continue planting fall and winter crops as space becomes available.
Week 39 21 September 27 September	**Garden Work**: Collect and dry herbs for winter use. Begin to plan next year's garden layout. **Sowing**: Last chance to sow quick-growing cool-season crops outdoors. **Transplanting**: Plant garlic cloves and shallots for harvesting next summer.
Week 40 28 September 04 October	**Garden Work**: Prepare for the first frost by having row covers ready for sensitive crops. **Sowing**: Indoors, start seeds for greens that will grow in the winter greenhouse or under grow lights. **Transplanting**: Plant perennial herbs and flowers that will establish over the cooler months.
Week 41 05 October 11 October	**Garden Work**: Continue harvesting warm-season crops before the first frost. Monitor for pests. **Sowing**: Directly sow leafy greens like spinach and mustard greens in cooler areas.
Week 42 12 October 18 October	**Garden Work**: Begin cleaning up garden beds and removing spent plants and debris. **Sowing**: Sow cover crops in beds that will be left fallow over winter. **Transplanting**: Plant garlic cloves and shallots for a summer harvest.

Week 43 19 October 25 October	**Garden Work**: Apply mulch to perennial beds to protect roots from temperature fluctuations. **Sowing**: Last chance to sow fast-growing, cool-weather crops in the warmest parts of the region. **Transplanting**: Plant strawberries for next spring's harvest.
Week 44 26 October 01 November	**Garden Work**: Set up frost protection strategies for tender perennials and winter crops. **Sowing**: Indoors, start herbs and greens in containers
Week 45 02 November 08 November	**Garden Work**: Collect and compost fallen leaves to create a rich soil amendment.
Week 46 09 November 15 November	**Garden Work**: Check stored vegetables and fruits for spoilage and use or remove any that are turning.
Week 47 16 November 22 November	**Garden Work**: Winterize irrigation systems and store gardening tools after cleaning.
Week 48 23 November 29 November	**Garden Work**: Plan next year's garden, considering crop rotation and new plant varieties.
Week 49 30 November 06 December	**Garden Work**: Decorate for the holidays with garden materials, such as holly, pinecones, and dried herbs.
Week 50 07 December 13 December	**Garden Work**: Ensure winter protection is in place for sensitive plants and young trees.
Week 51 14 December 20 December	**Garden Work**: Review garden notes from the past year to plan improvements for the next season.
Week 52 21 December 27 December	**Garden Work**: Take time to rest and enjoy the holiday season. Reflect on the garden's successes and lessons learned over the past year.

Made in the USA
Monee, IL
25 November 2024

71151535R00079